A Place to Start

Stories and Essays from Down the Road

Jim Grey

A Place to Start

Stories and Essays from Down the Road

Jim Grey

ISBN 978-1-7360571-0-0

Midnight Star Press

Contents

Introduction

I needed a hobby. Money was tight. Blogging was free.

I wanted to write about the brutal end of my destructive marriage. I needed to process it, make sense of it.

But I wouldn't write directly about what happened. I had stories to tell about my ex, real humdingers. It would have been cathartic to tell them! But she had humdingers to tell about me, too. I wouldn't like her doing that, not in such a public way. I wasn't going to do it to her.

We met in church when I was 24. She was lithe and athletic, head-strong and oustpoken. I fell hard, fast. She wasn't as sure – she was a little older than me, previously married with a young son. Her stakes were higher. But I pursued her and soon we were a couple, and then we were married. I was 27. I thought we had built a solid connection in our dating years, but from the start of our marriage we struggled to gain our footing. She was critical; I withdrew. She chased after me; I withdrew harder. In the end, we were both furious that our dreams had not been fulfilled, and we both acted out in our anger in our own ways. Our anger did damage that we couldn't fix.

Our sons were young when I moved out, just five and seven. I had wanted to be their dad in every little thing, to have lots of time to enjoy them and share experiences with them, to guide them when those moments presented themselves. When my marriage ended, so did the days with my sons. I got to see them only sometimes, on the schedule the judge created. It ripped me apart.

I ached in my bones, in my skin. I wanted to run away, to withdraw for months and return recovered, refreshed. But I couldn't. My sons needed me there to help them through this loss, to make a new and happy home for us for the time we had with each other. I had to keep working to pay the mortgage and the child support.

Instead I wrote stories of my life, from childhood and early adulthood as well as from the then present day. I shared my positions about topics I believed in. And I wrote about my faith. My divorce could have caused me to lose my faith, but I'm a stubborn man and I intended to hold God to what I thought were his promises. All of this writing helped me process my life and what had happened.

I started my blog, *Down the Road*, on February 7, 2007. If you read my blog today – and I hope you do, at blog.jimgrey.net – you probably know me as a film photographer or as that fellow who documents abandoned roads. But I've always woven in essays and stories from my life. These posts seldom get the most pageviews, but in comments readers tell me how much they love these posts.

This book collects most of the stories and essays I wrote in my blog's first two years. They show that neither I nor my blog had fully found our voices yet. But I had started. There is so much power in starting. From there, you can find your way. You can't find your way until you start.

With this book I start my publishing journey. Who knows where it will take me? I get to enjoy finding my way with it, just as I still enjoy finding my way with my blog. Just as, now that I can look back on it, I enjoyed building a new life after my marriage ended.

Blogging for so many years has made me a much better writer. As I laid these stories and essays into this book, I revised them all to better tell my story and to make it more interesting.

I think everybody's life is interesting – yours too. It's all in how you tell the stories. I'm an ordinary man with an ordinary life, but these stories together form a memoir that tells how rich even an ordinary life can be.

Acknowledgements

Thanks to Johanna Rothman for inflicting help. Thanks to Katherine Magee for letting me use her photo on the cover, Damion Grey for letting me use his photo of me in the back of the book, and to Robyn Weber for letting me use a photo her mother took when we were all kids (rest in peace, Judy Dieu). Thanks to Dave Jenkins and Mike Pressley for reading an early draft and offering valuable feedback. Thanks to my wife Margaret for always encouraging me.

Stories

My dad had a hard childhood in the hills of West Virginia during and after World War II – his mother died, his dad drank too much, he was raised by a grandmother who loved him but was very busy with her own life. He seldom talked about it while I was growing up. It's strange to remember that now, because the last 25 years or so of his life were so characterized by him telling his life's stories over and over.

You'd think my childhood would have featured several trips home to the hills, but no. Dad seemed content to leave that part of his life behind him. In 1990, when I was 23 and he was 49, I convinced him to make a father-son trip back to that little railroad town down Highway 61 from Charleston, and I finally got to see the hardscrabble railroad-and-coal town where my father came from.

As Dad entered his 50s, his last child graduated and left home and his father's generation aged and died. It was probably no coincidence that during these years Dad started to tell his stories. They were rough; details and sometimes outcomes changed with each telling. But by his early 60s, when Dad became the oldest surviving member of the family, his stories were complete. He told them the same way for the rest of his life. I am sure that through telling his stories he made sense of his difficult youth. Through them, he found peace. That made it possible for him reconnect with the Greys still in the hills, and we returned several times before he died.

In my 40s, to make sense of and find peace with my own past difficulties I began to write my own life stories. I've published most of them on my blog; a few I keep close to the vest. But as I did that work I kept thinking about my father's stories. Through them I came to see just the tragedy and pain he suffered and how it shaped him. It allowed me to have great empathy for him.

Telling my own stories, making sense of my life, has allowed me to have great empathy for myself.

Welcome to Thorntown

My blog was less than a week old when I wrote this post. Still hurting badly from the end of my marriage, I thought it might help if I wrote a story about a good memory of that relationship. Sadly, there weren't many to choose from; our marriage was difficult from the start. I had to go back to when we were dating to find a happy story. Still, writing this story was good for my spirit.

State Road 47 is a winding and lovely drive in western Indiana. It begins in the wild terrain around Turkey Run State Park. As it heads east, those steep hills become the rolling terrain of quiet farmland. The road curves frequently around old farm boundaries and around terrain challenges. But the fun ends at Thorntown as the road straightens out for the rest of its route to Sheridan, thirty minutes north of Indianapolis.

Thorntown, a well-kept small town lined with tidy homes, churches, and shops, is at the center of what was briefly the 64,000-acre Thorntown Indian Reserve, where the Eel River Tribe of the Miami Indians lived. Thorntown gets its name from the Miami name for the place, Kawiakiungi, which means "place of thorns." It's an old-fashioned Indiana small town where everybody knows everybody. At any moment, you expect it to start snowing, and Jimmy Stewart to come running through town shouting, "Merry Christmas you wonderful old Building and Loan!"

As much as I have always liked State Road 47, I used to dislike Thorntown because its 30 mph speed limit interrupted my swift progress. When my ex-wife and I were dating many years ago, she and I passed through Thorntown on our way to a camping trip. We needed both of our small cars to haul all the gear. She followed me.

As usual, I didn't see the speed limit signs at the edge of town, but this time the law was ready for me. A police car pulled out of somebody's driveway with lights flashing and siren blaring. I pulled over and the officer, a big Sheriff Buford type with the buzz cut and the mirrored aviator sunglasses, began to give me a chewin' out. His face pinched, he was wondering with considerable volume if I had skill enough to read speed-limit signs when my now-ex, who by the way was lovely and slender with blue-grey eyes and a big mess of blonde hair, pulled around in front of me and stopped. Sheriff Buford seemed annoyed and waddled purposefully toward her car. He was gone for quite some time, but when he came back, he was chuckling and smiling. He told me to just take it slow through town and wished me a good weekend!

This happened before everybody had cell phones. I had to wait about two hours until we reached our campsite to ask just what the heck happened. She said, "When he came up, I rolled down the window, batted my eyelashes at him, and said, 'If you give him a ticket, you have to give me one too, because I was following him!' He laughed and laughed and I guessed when you drove off that he let us off the hook."

This did not do anything to improve my opinion about Thorntown.

I've matured considerably since then. I've also become much better at noticing the speed limit signs at the outskirts of small towns, so I'm much less likely to attract police attention. So now I not only bear no ill will against Thorntown, but I find its entrance from the east to be quite lovely. You swing around this little curve and over a small bridge, and then suddenly the town unfolds before you, as if it had been folded snugly into the pages of a pop-up book. Just be sure to be going 30 mph when you get there!

12 February 2007

Restored in Bridgeton

In my early 20s not only was I out of school but I was working at things I'd long dreamed about. I made my living making software, and had a part-time gig playing music on the radio. You'd think I would feel like I was on top of the world, but somehow achieving these dreams just didn't fulfill me. I was lonely; I became depressed.

When I felt the walls of my Terre Haute apartment closing in on me I distracted myself by driving out in the country. One day I drove the back roads out of Terre Haute into southern Parke County and soon began seeing handmade signs pointing to Bridgeton. I was curious, so I followed the signs. The Bridgeton Road wound long, then abruptly entered a little town. Before I could even take it in, the road just as abruptly came upon a covered bridge.

I parked. It was still but for the wind and for water rushing beneath the bridge. Some of the structures looked like they came out of a wild-west movie, especially an old mill and what looked like a general store. I wondered whether the town was abandoned until I noticed some homes that, while in need of maintenance, had at some time been updated with vinyl siding and double-pane windows.

Even though the bridge was on the town's northern edge, it was clearly the centerpiece, better cared for than anything around it. It needed a little attention — a coat of paint, a couple missing boards replaced — but was otherwise in excellent shape, especially considering "1868" was painted over the entrance arch. It stood there sure, as if it thought it was the reason the town continued to exist. It seemed not to need traffic (the road had been rerouted over a concrete bridge) or even admirers to be self-sufficient.

I walked the bridge and admired it. I was delighted by its design. I could see the fingerprints of its designer and builder (J. J. Daniels, also painted over the arch) in the beams that fanned from the foundation to the roof and the regularly spaced trusses that connected its east side to its west. As I walked, the bridge stood solid, without shimmying, shaking, or groaning. The designer meant this bridge to last. And even after it was bypassed by a newer bridge, others clearly valued the designer's desire and kept it in good repair.

Standing on the bridge and thinking of the men who built it and cared for it soothed, calmed, and encouraged me. It put me in touch with the good people can do when something matters to them. It showed me that some things can last.

Bridgeton was my ace in the hole for my toughest times. I never remembered the way, so I just drove vaguely north into the country until I found the signs. The trips were like going to the well for a drink of peace, and I always went home comforted and refreshed.

Soon I moved away from Terre Haute. Years passed, and I never made it back to Bridgeton. Then in 2005 somebody set fire to the bridge, destroying it. I didn't realize until the arson that so many other people had a large soft spot in their heart for this place and its bridge. Emotions flowed freely as many people mourned the loss of their old friend. Out of this pain, locals immediately decided to rebuild. A new bridge was finished just in time for the 2006 Covered Bridge Festival, an annual celebration of all of Parke County's 31 covered bridges.

I had a day to myself late that October, after the Covered Bridge Festival had ended, and found myself out that way. It had been 15 years since I'd last visited Bridgeton, and I decided to detour to see the new bridge. I was anxious. I was going to see that my old friend was gone, replaced by something new. But I was eager, too, to see how the new bridge turned out.

As usual, I drove around until I found the signs pointing to Bridgeton. Soon enough I entered town, and there she was. She wasn't an exact replica of the old bridge, but she was mighty close. (All of these photos are of the new bridge.) I felt like my old friend had never left. The designers and builders put great effort and care into rebuilding this bridge. Their fingerprints are in the two arches that span each side, and in the beams and trusses that keep her square. She is absolutely gorgeous. The postcard shot was always from the north to include the little waterfall, and now is no exception.

That this bridge isn't a carbon copy of her ancestor doesn't seem to matter. What made the old bridge special was the spirit of the people who made it, the very humanity their efforts gave it. Such spirit was captured when she was rebuilt. She may be brand new, but it's like she's never been gone. And I left feeling comforted and refreshed, just like always.

13 February 2007

A good icing

I grew up in South Bend, Indiana, in the 1970s. Back then, snow was on the ground from November through April. It seemed like there was always enough snow for forts or snowball fights. But I lost my love for snow at age nine when I was first issued a shovel and told to clear the driveway. It was common to need to shovel two or three times a day for several days at a stretch. The cold was always a real worry, too. Mom wasn't being overprotective when she ordered hats, gloves, hoods, and scarves. I remember walking to and from school in winds so strong and cold that I would sometimes walk for blocks sideways, legs braced, so my back could take the brunt.

When I moved to Terre Haute for college, the relatively mild winters made that west-central Indiana city seem like a distant foreign land. Snows always melted within a few days, and I could run around with an unzipped coat and no hat.

Terre Haute's signature winter move was the ice storm. They always made the roads treacherous and brought down power lines. But if you had power and didn't have to go anywhere, you could go outside and take in the beauty the storms left behind. Everything was coated in a layer of ice, which made ordinary things such as trees and street signs and fences sparkle fresh and clean — and stiff. I remember driving down I-70 on my way back to college a couple days after an ice storm. The trees lining the road looked like ghosts as their white-tipped branches hung low and still.

I got a job in Terre Haute after college. After an ice storm that first winter, I chipped a half-inch of ice off my car and slowly drove the slippery roads to work. I passed by the beauty the storm left behind: glistening trees and rows of little icicles hanging off power lines and street signs. I also had to drive around the storm's destruction of downed power lines and fallen trees and branches.

I found my co-workers sitting around the cold, dark breakroom drinking gas-station coffee. The power company couldn't say when power would be restored. I knew that even after power returned it would take hours for the computer servers I depended on to all come back up. I didn't want to shiver in the breakroom all day, so I drove back home, found my camera, and walked a block to Collett Park to take these photos. My photography skills were weak, but I think these photos turned out all right.

I came upon this young oak near the horseshoe club's pit. The tree must not have been too strong, given that it was propped up like that. But its leaves were awfully tenacious, still clinging to the tree well into winter. Even the ice storm's strong winds couldn't break these leaves free. Instead, the ice conformed itself to the leaves.

The mature trees, having long ago lost their leaves, glowed in a quarter-inch coating of ice.

The ice weighed the branches down, making them hang low.

The nets on the tennis court glistened, frozen stiff.

The coarse ice down the center of a curved slide would have made for a rough ride.

The fence looked like a Photoshop "unsharp mask" effect had been applied to it — except that nobody had heard of Photoshop yet.

The storm also left ice appearing to drip off the clothesline and power lines in my back yard.

I had a lovely time that morning with my camera. I stopped only because my fingers grew numb in the cold!

26 February 2007

A place to start

Only the rough neighborhoods fit my budget. I'd just graduated from engineering school in Terre Haute and had landed a job in town, but times were tough and the pay was poor.

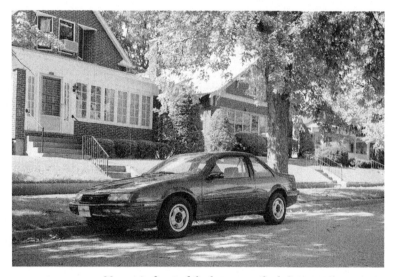

My car in front of the house, on the left

On the way to see an apartment on the wrong side of the tracks, I passed through the tree-lined Collett Park neighborhood with its American Foursquare and Craftsman Bungalow houses. Built for a growing middle class around the turn of the century, it was a cheerful, well-kept neighborhood of sidewalks and wide front porches. I admired its tightly packed homes as I drove slowly down one of its concrete streets. I noticed a For Rent sign in the front window of a tall house wrapped in asphalt sheeting styled to look like brick. Even though I doubted I could afford this neighborhood, I stopped and rang the bell.

A large, gruff man in a thin, wrinkled, v-neck T-shirt and gray chinos came to the door and looked me over. I asked about the apartment and he disappeared to find the key. He showed me around the side to the entrance. As soon as I entered, I was sure that I couldn't afford the place. It was clean. Hardwood floors glowed subtly around the room's edge, framing fresh rugs. The walls were recently painted or wallpapered. The large, gruff man, who finally introduced himself as Steve, had clearly cared for the place.

Suspicious of this wide-eyed kid, Steve began to size me up by asking where I went to school. When I said Rose-Hulman, which is a well-regarded engineering school on the edge of town, his voice rose a note toward tentatively cheerful. He said he went there, too, back before the war when it was still called Rose Poly, but he couldn't hack it and went on to work 30 years at the post office. He talked as he led me through, alternating between Rose stories and calling out one or two features of each room.

I was glad he was talking because I was excited and didn't want to betray it. A built-in cabinet and chest of drawers consumed half of one of the bedroom's walls. In the enormous bathroom, white porcelain tile covered the walls to four feet high. Original antique fixtures were still in place, including a claw-foot tub and a sink with separate hot and cold taps. In the kitchen, an early-1950s Tappan electric stove, gleaming in white and chrome, stood across from a long, shallow farmhouse sink. A built-in table and benches filled a tiny breakfast nook. French doors led the way from the living room to the den. The woodwork was 12 inches tall with corner posts, and the doorknobs were either glass or ornate brass ovals. By this time Steve was telling me that he bought the house in 1935 after he married his wife Henrietta, that it was almost 100 years old, and that the original owner had built the apartment for his mother-in-law by blocking off three rooms of the house and adding the kitchen and den.

The path to the front door

The history charmed me as I noticed some of the place's short-comings. The hallway wallpaper had a hideous check pattern with large bright yellow flowers, the bathroom walls above the porcelain tile were painted bright pink, I would have to supply my own refrigerator, the house had one furnace and Steve controlled the temperature, and Steve made clear that tenants could have all the friends over they wanted as long as they were white.

I wanted the place. I decided I could live with the faults and I would cross the color line should it become necessary. I drew a breath, sure he was going to set a price beyond my budget, and said, "I like it. How much?"

Steve drew back and narrowed his eyes at me for a minute. He said he'd had a lot of trouble with recent tenants; he had just evicted a "coupla girls from Indiana State" for having a string of different men staying overnight. He wondered aloud if I could afford it and if I would cause him any trouble. He examined me — and in that instant I was sure that he was setting the rent just outside what he thought I could afford. After a long pause that made me fidget, he barked: "250."

I reeled, dizzy with disbelief. That was less than what I'd pay for a dump in the rough neighborhoods! "I'll take it," I said quietly. He leaned well into my personal space, frowning. "Are you sure? I said the rent is $250." I pulled my checkbook out of my back pocket and said, "I can pay the first month's rent right now." He backed off, took the check, shook my hand, and that was that. I had a home.

I can't imagine renting on a handshake today, but I lucked into a great situation. Steve and Henrietta were honorable people who stayed out of my business and kept the apartment in good repair. They even got rid of the pink bathroom walls, peeling away nine layers of wallpaper under that paint and laying in new subtly patterned wallpaper in a much less garish tan.

Sadly, Steve passed away within the year. After that, Henrietta took care of things herself. "If you're happy, I'm happy," she said to me several times, and never raised my rent.

I could furnish the place only sparsely at first. I owned a bed, a dresser, a desk, and a broken black-and-white console TV. I bought a recliner and some tables at a used furniture store. I accepted charity from Mom. Soon I had the place suitably appointed.

I started building my budding adult life in my little place, and invited my friends in. My girlfriend spent many of her evenings there with me, relaxing, watching TV, talking, sharing companionship and company. My parents drove to town for a visit from time to time. My brother would drive to town and we'd go out for drinks, or an old college friend would come up from Louisville and we'd get carryout and watch movies all night. An old girlfriend came to see me from Bloomington, and a dear old friend flew in once from Toronto. I had a close friend and some of her friends over for a toast of sorts when she graduated from St. Mary-of-the-Woods. I even made a nice dinner for my boss, his girlfriend, and my girlfriend. We all squeezed into the little breakfast nook to eat. My little apartmet was at the center of many of my activities and so of my world.

The living room

But I'd soon suffer some sad and lonely years. My relationship with the first girlfriend fell apart at about the same time another friendship ended very painfully. These passages let me see some ways I wasn't healthy in my relationships. Most of my other friends were graduating and moving away, and I found it hard to make new friends. I felt lost and stuck; I grew depressed. I used to beat myself up over not working harder to push past these challenges. Fortunately, I have since forgiven myself for being human.

I took lots of long drives to escape my feelings, but at the end I always had to go home and face myself. In that, my apartment was a blessing for reasons beyond the hardwood floors, the low rent, and the good landlord: it was a comfortable and safe place learn to be me. I did a lot of things there that I enjoyed and that helped me figure out who I was and what I liked. I taught myself how to cook. I watched a lot of late-night cable in the dark with a beer in my hand. I lay on the floor in the den listening to album after album, singing along at the top of my lungs, thankful that Henrietta was hard of hearing.

Comfortable in my home

In time I made some friends, good ones. Still, I frequently wished for companionship, thinking that it would make the rest of my problems go away. When I found companionship, to my confusion the rest of my problems were still there. I found myself unable to make things better on my own. I entered therapy for the first time. And I started looking for God. I'd never sought him before, but my problems were bigger than I was and I figured if anyone could handle them, the creator of the universe could.

The seeds of change were planted in me in that apartment. Between God and therapy, I began to heal where I was wrong and see where I was all right to begin with. I started to learn how to be content with my circumstances even when they're not ideal. Those days tried to show me, though I still struggle with this lesson, that part of humanity's core beauty lies in its limitations and its imperfections.

For more than 20 years, when my days were troubled my dreams were filled with this apartment. It represented comfort and a place where difficult things can happen safely. I still miss the place.

The house in 2007, needing TLC

When I'm in Terre Haute, I try to drive through the old neighborhood. The last time was a few years ago. I found the house now sided in gray vinyl, the concrete steps beginning to crumble, the painted trim peeling, the hedges overgrown. Much was the case up and down the block, all of which showed these early signs of decline. Houses in neighboring blocks showed serious neglect. The neighborhood was becoming rough.

By that time, Henrietta's health declined to the point where she had to sell the house and move into assisted living, after having lived on that street all her life.

Henrietta's life moved on, and so must mine. But still, whenever I'm in town I drive by. I always want to park and go in. I would probably be surprised not to see my brown recliner there, the TV remote on the arm, waiting for me to sit and watch the evening news.

9 March 2007

I like cameras

I gave up all of my hobbies during my first marriage. Our lives were busy and the relationship was hard. I thought I needed to give all of my time to my family. It was a terrible mistake. Having something interesting to work on that's all mine is a critical way I renew myself to be present with the people I love.

My parents were sure I was headed toward a career in engineering because I liked figuring out how things worked. I could hardly keep my fingers off anything with buttons or knobs. I messed up a few things as a kid by pushing buttons and turning knobs.

My great grandmother had an incredibly old TV, and behind this panel right at kid height were about a million knobs. Whenever we visited, if I found myself alone with that TV I turned as many of them as I could before being discovered. This almost certainly caused her to utter choice words when she settled in that night to watch *Gunsmoke.*

I ruined my Grandpa's new clock radio by turning one apparently important knob past its stop point. Grandma asked me many times if I did it, but I didn't have the guts to admit it. Grandma kept a closer watch over me after that. Grandpa got a CB radio as a part of that fad in the late 1970s. Grandma took me aside, pointed to the knob labeled SQUELCH, and said, "Jimmy, now, if you turn that knob, it will explode!" It was several years before I figured out that was a scam.

The summer I turned nine, my brother and I took our first annual summer trip spend a couple weeks at our grandparents' home on a little lake in southwestern Michigan. One day we were out riding in Grandma's truck on the main highway when she stopped for a yard sale. There I found a little Kodak Brownie Starmite II, an inexpensive plastic fixed-focus camera from the early 1960s that took roll film. I picked it up and turned it over and over, fascinated.

I'd never really handled a camera before, unless you count one day when I was about four years old. We were on a family trip. I picked up Mom's camera and took about 10 photos of our hotel room — the doorknob, the corner of the bed, the wall, and so on. I felt so grown up with that camera, but when Mom discovered me, boy was I ever in trouble!

That memory wasn't even in my mind as I tried to figure out that Brownie. Grandma came by and saw me playing with it and asked, "Do you want that?" I was quite embarrassed to have been noticed, and I stammered something noncommittal like, "Oh, no, I don't know, not really." Grandma noticed the 25-cent price tag, looked me square in the eye in that way she did that said firmly, "I see right through you," and silently handed me a quarter. I was both embarrassed and relieved because I really did want that camera.

I explored that Brownie the rest of the time I was at Grandma's. I learned how to open it and how to wind it. I pressed my eye to the open bottom of the camera and pressed the shutter to see light flash into the camera for a fraction of a second. I looked at the camera's face, pressed the button, and saw the shutter open and close almost imperceptibly. I was fascinated with the camera's intricacy and with all the thought and work that had gone into designing it.

When I got home, I bought a roll of film and tried it out. The neighborhood kids made me the center of attention; they all wanted to be in a picture. They also all wanted to hold the camera and look at it and take pictures with it, though I drew the line there since my roll of film held just 12 exposures and I had spent a month's allowance to buy it. When we next went grocery shopping, I dropped the exposed roll off at the nearby drug store for developing. When the photos came back, the developing and printing set me back a dizzying three months' allowance! But I was the neighborhood's center of attention all over again when I brought the developed photos home. I must have given most of the photos away because I have only four prints today. Here's one of those prints: Darin, Colleen, Christy, David, Mike, a shirtless boy who I don't recognize as his face is blocked, and Craig running into the frame. They were all happy to pose for my camera.

I owned other cameras. A twin-lens Brownie Reflex Synchro Model with flash holder found its way into my hands. Then Dad bought me a new Instamatic knockoff. Later, Grandma and Grandpa gave me a new Polaroid instant camera for Christmas. But I didn't start to deliberately collect cameras until I was a teenager and could go find them.

My Saturday mornings became filled with yard sales. I used to ride my bike to them all over South Bend's southeast side. Most of the cameras I found were simple Instamatics and the like and cost a buck or less. But then one day I came across an Argus A-Four 35mm camera that, as a manual-focus camera, had more stuff to figure out on it than I'd ever seen. I parted with the painfully dear sum of four dollars to buy it. I felt like I had scored the coup of the century! It took me quite some time to figure that camera out, with help from a friend with some photography skill who taught me a little about exposure and focus. Eventually I filled it with film and shot a few rolls. It became and remained a favorite camera.

I kept this up through my teens and early 20s. Whenever I got a new camera, just like with my first one I'd spend happy hours figuring it out. By the time I was 25, I owned more than 100 cameras — a bunch of Brownies, a few movie cameras, a dozen Polaroids, some box cameras, several old folding cameras, and too many crappy Instamatics. I took photos with a few of the cameras. Other cameras' picture-taking days were clearly over.

After I married and had children, I displayed all of my folding cameras on the fireplace mantle. My sons asked to look at them, and although I was reluctant at first, I eventually relented. None of my cameras was worth so much that any kid damage would really matter anyway. I showed the boys how they worked — how to open them, set them so that the shutter would fire, put their eye up to the opening to watch light flash into the camera when they pressed the shutter. They had great fun looking them over. That encouraged me to get out my boxes of cameras for us all to play with. Over the years, we spent many pleasant hours on the living room floor playing with my cameras. I put a roll of film into a Kodak 35mm camera in my collection and took it and my sons out into the yard. We had great fun together that afternoon making photographs of each other. The prints I had made are a lovely reminder of the good feelings we shared that day.

As my marriage faltered and ended, I needed to shed most of my possessions. My camera collection did not survive the culling. Unexpectedly, I did not miss most of them. But I still wish I had a couple cameras that I especially enjoyed using, and a few cameras that friends and family gave me as gifts.

Still, after all these years I have not lost my fascination with things that require careful design, and I remain fascinated with even the cheapest, simplest camera. I decided to start a new collection, this time buying only cameras for which film is still made, that are in good cosmetic condition, and that still work. Ultimately, I'd like to shoot at least one roll of film in each camera I buy.

eBay has dramatically changed how I can collect cameras. Every day, hundreds of vintage cameras are available. No more yard sales! I have already bought two cameras online. I'm excited to see where this leads!

17 March 2007

Home alone

My ex-wife was happiest when she was busy, and so she always had an astonishing to-do list going. Saturday mornings she'd bounce out of bed at six and work hard and fast all day, with a million things to do. She reminded me of the episode of *Gilligan's Island* where Mrs. Howell ate the radioactive sugar beets and cleaned her hut at warp speed.

Before marriage I had been used to leisurely Saturdays and tried to convert my wife, but she'd have none of it. She told me that she knew she kept busier than two or three people and didn't expect me to match her pace. But still I felt a little guilty about my sloth.

The house I rented then, showing just a portion of its large yard

Partly from that guilt and partly from seeing that our older home and large yard needed attention, I eventually started making my own Saturday to-do lists. Mine were a fraction of hers, but it seemed like my tasks always filled the day. And while I worked, our sons would run around in the yard, watch cartoons, and ask me for a drink or for lunch. Our dogs would chase squirrels around the back yard. And the neighbors behind us would often come to the fence to hand me a leftover loaf of challah from the bakery where they worked. Man, we loved that challah! And I loved our family life. But I never loved those hardworking Saturdays.

When my wife and I separated, I immediately reverted to more leisurely Saturdays. But where I used to be able to sleep until 10 or 11, now I can't sleep past 8. And where in my pre-marriage days I could fill an entire Saturday hanging out with friends, watching movies on TV, or just running around, now I'm likely to clean a bathroom, cut the grass, and do my grocery shopping first. Actually, before I married, I neglected the regular chores. I guess my ex-wife's hyper-productive behavior rubbed off on me for the good.

So now that I can work as little or as much as I decide to on Saturday, I miss the kids, the dogs, and the neighbors. I'm sure my problem is common among divorced men — adjusting to being alone so much. My sons are here every other weekend, playing with Legos, exploring the large property on which I live, watching cartoons, and playing video games. I put off the chores and just try to enjoy the time with them. Sometimes we'll go to the park or the dollar store, or we'll drive up north to visit Grandma and Grandpa, or just play Clue or Monopoly at the dining table with plenty of snacks. It's not idyllic; the boys bicker and scrape their knees and get upset when I say no, just like in most families. But we have good times overall.

I haven't been separated from my family for all that long. The Saturdays I spend alone are long and maddeningly quiet. At first I filled those days with things to do that, although enjoyable, mostly kept me from having to face my loneliness. But all that activity merely wore me out and used up my reserves. Lately I have tried to stay home more and just face the quiet. I itched with anxiety the first few Saturdays I tried it. My mind raced with thoughts of escape. If a friend had called to say, "Let's go see a movie," I probably would have jumped twenty feet across the room to grab my car keys.

Eventually I decided just simply to let myself be anxious, whether I liked it or not. After a few more solitary Saturdays, the feeling started to pass. As I faced the quiet, empty house, my serenity and sense of centeredness began to grow. I began to feel that I'm okay just the way things are. To my surprise, this has helped me be more present with my sons when they are here!

Even though I'm coming to terms with being alone, sometimes while I'm mopping the kitchen or making out my grocery list on a solitary Saturday, I startle and feel a strong urge to quickly go find the boys since they've been quiet for so long! I'll be glad when I can just chuckle at myself when I do that.

18 March 2007

Brushes with greatness

19 years old with my first wheels

In the summer of 1986 I drove a rusty brown Ford Pinto all over
northern Indiana delivering small packages for my aunt Betty's
courier service. The Pinto was basic transportation; its only creature
comfort was an AM radio. I left it tuned to WLS in Chicago, which
still played top-40 music then. Fred Winston did the morning show,
Don Wade and his wife Roma held down middays, and Larry
Lujack and Rich McMillan came on in the afternoon. They were
such fun to listen to!

I can't remember which of them had the call-in feature called
"Brushes with Greatness," in which listeners were invited to call and
tell touching and funny stories of times they encountered famous
people. For a guy who has always lived in places famous people
studiously avoid, I've encountered a surprising number of people

of talent and notoriety. These, then, are my brushes with greatness.

I admit that this first story is a stretch. My parents played cards with their best friends, the Porters, every Saturday night for more than 40 years. Somehow, Mr. Porter knew Tony Randall, a well-known actor who most famously played Felix Unger on the sitcom *The Odd Couple*. One Saturday night sometime in the late 70s, dragged along to the Porters' for another night of watching TV until the adults quit playing cards, the air was electric because Mr. Randall was expected to call. The phone soon rang, and while Mr. Porter and Mr. Randall talked I sat in wonder that this man I watched in reruns was alive at his telephone. Did he stand at the wall phone in his kitchen like Mr. Porter? Or did he rather sit in a cordovan leather wing chair in a book-lined study with a half-consumed glass of tawny port next to his black desk phone on an oval walnut end table with red oak inlay? Mr. Porter seemed a little taller to me for a while after that call.

Here's a much better story. In the summer of 1985, I met a bunch of friends from all corners of Indiana on a Lake Michigan beach near Michigan City for a weekend of beaching and catching up with each other. We were all young and stupid, and Indiana hadn't passed any seat-belt laws yet, so we got the bright idea to cram ourselves into a little Nissan hatchback and go for a drive. Nine of us somehow fit into that car. We put the windows down and cruised, enjoying the warm summer air.

At a light a dark BMW sedan with dark windows pulled up alongside us. We all oohed and aahed over the shiny Bimmer when the front passenger window went down. A man leaned across the seat and asked us for directions to a movie theater. He looked familiar, and his voice was distinctive, but it wasn't until our driver asked in disbelief, "Are you Jim Belushi?" that it clicked. He quickly said yes, but immediately asked again for directions. The girl sitting in my lap lived in the area and started to shout the directions as the light changed and the rest of us in the car went nuts. Both cars pulled away, directions still being shouted. We were going pretty fast by the time Jim thanked us, rolled up his window, and zoomed away. I learned later that the Belushis owned property nearby, in a wealthy beach enclave.

Dad's friend Mr. Porter directed the art museum at the University of Notre Dame, and we got invited to a whole bunch of exhibit openings. I met many of the artists, the ones who were still living, anyway. The only one to leave any impression on me was Christo. He and his wife Jeanne-Claude do big and sometimes controversial works such as wrapping the German Reichstag in over a million square feet of polypropylene in or hanging saffron-colored strips of cloth from saffron-colored vinyl poles in New York's Central Park.

Christo's entrance sent electric ripples through the room. The man had his own atmosphere! I felt the air grow thinner as he approached Mr. Porter, next to whom I was standing. Mr. Porter introduced me. Christo didn't look directly at me as he extended a hand — the dampest, most flaccid handshake of my life.

I didn't exactly meet Richard Carpenter, but I got a letter from him. I've always loved the Carpenters' music, and sometime during my college years I wrote a gushing letter to the Carpenters Fan Club telling them so. A couple months later a letter came for me in an envelope marked with the A&M Records logo. It contained a brief letter from Richard on A&M letterhead saying that my letter touched him. His long signature looked like a convention of ovals. I have to believe it was a form letter handed to Richard for signature, but I was thrilled anyway. I sure wish I knew what happened to that letter.

In college, my friend Michael was music director for the campus radio station. He built relationships with record-company reps, who sometimes sent him swag and invited him to concerts to encourage him to play their artists' songs on the air. He got invited to a heavy-metal triple bill in Chicago and asked me along: Armored Saint, Grim Reaper, and power-metal pioneers Helloween. I'm sure you don't know these bands, but they were a big deal to us! I liked Armored Saint and Grim Reaper all right and I was hot into Helloween. Sweetening the deal, Michael got invited to interview the founder of Grim Reaper, a guitarist named Nick Bowcott.

We drove from Terre Haute in Michael's old Buick, a $750 car stuffed with $1,500 of premium audio equipment. We rocked powerfully and distortion-free all the way to the venue only to find that the show had been moved to a bar in some other part of town. I thought we were sunk, but Michael was not daunted. He followed some sketchy directions, threading his leviathan automobile through narrow streets in seedy parts of town, and we made the show just in time. It rocked.

Afterwards, we were escorted to the tour bus where Nick awaited. The whole band was on board, along with a stream of girls right around the age of consent with faces full of makeup, bodies not very full of clothes, and eyes full of hope and desire that they would be special that night. Band members seemed at once interested, wary, and uncomfortable with their attention — except the lead singer, who just seemed interested.

Most of the girls were shooed off. Nick sat down before us, Michael pressed the Record button on his little tape recorder, and the interview began. Nick was bright, energetic, passionate, and engaged. He answered Michael's questions thoughtfully and thoroughly, talking freely about the band, making albums, succeeding in the recording industry, and even the existence of God (which he doubted). He looked deeply and intensely into our eyes as he spoke. Didn't he know we were just two 20-year-old kids from a 160-watt radio station in Terre Haute, Indiana? He treated us like we were from Rolling Stone and gave us his sole attention for as long as Michael had questions. Nick Bowcott was a class act.

Finally, I got to see one of my favorite bands, Heart, play in 2006 at a fine old theater in South Bend. I was stoked: I had won a contest to briefly meet Ann and Nancy Wilson backstage before the show. The other contest winners and I waited near the stage entrance for our chance. The handler came out and said that our meeting would be very brief and that we could have them sign one item each. I hadn't thought to bring something to autograph! A friendly woman with a bright smile asked me if I would mind having Ann and Nancy sign an item she brought, since she had brought two.

As the handler took us backstage, he explained that we would do this in receiving-line style so we wouldn't overwhelm Ann and Nancy. We were to quietly wait our turn or we would be escorted out, period. The air grew tense as Ann and Nancy came out, flanked by crew. They stayed shoulder to shoulder with each other and looked about anxiously. They dutifully signed the items we brought but didn't say anything. When my turn came, I told her how much pleasure her music had brought me. She looked confused for a moment, but shortly it registered what I had said. She looked me in the eye and said with surprise, in a throaty voice, "Thank you. Thank you very much."

Ann signed what I had in my hands and looked directly at the person in line behind me, so I took the hint and moved over in front of Nancy. She just took my item and began to sign it without looking up. I wasn't sure what to say now, given that things had been so confused with Ann, so I just tried to catch her eyes. She finally noticed and looked at me. Her eyes were as blue as a spring sky, startlingly lovely — but her pupils were the size of sharp pencil points, tiny dots roaring that there would be no friendly chitchat. I mumbled that it was a pleasure to meet her, and then stepped toward the handler and waited until everybody had their turn. After the handler took a photo of us all, we were escorted back to the lobby.

Why didn't I think to get a photo with Nick Bowcott?

11 April 2007

Re-integrating joy

My dad once told me that I was the most joyful little boy he had ever known. During my first few years, he said, I constantly wore a big beaming smile and everything seemed to make me happy. The few memories I have of my first four years seem to support his perception.

My dad and me in 1970

Here are all of those memories:

First, I watched on TV as Apollo 11 landed on the moon. I don't remember the landing, but I do remember that it was sponsored by Gulf Oil with its big red-circle logo and its name within. Mom says that at every commercial break, I pointed at the screen and exclaimed, "Gulf!"

Next, I used to get up when Dad's alarm went off at 5 a.m., go quietly into my parents' room, and lie still on the corner of their bed in the dark. The radio played softly, always on the Hit Parade station, while Dad dressed for work. I heard Karen Carpenter sing and when I closed my eyes her voice made me see colors that flowed and shifted with her song. I hoped to hear her song every morning.

Finally, I woke up in the hospital after surgery groggy and angry, but very glad when Dad came to take me home. He picked me up and, as I moved through the air on my way to his chest, my anger faded. I felt secure way up there with my head on his shoulder, looking down at the recovery room. He says that I said to him, "They're not doing that to me again!"

These memories suggest to me that I took life as it was and easily experienced the feelings that went with it. No wonder I found it easy to feel joy. I *felt* easily.

My next memories, much more vivid and detailed, are of Kindergarten. My school looked like a castle in red brick trimmed in white with a slate roof and copper gutters. Room 001 was just inside the east entrance, and although the room had two entrance doors, you had to go in the far door because the near door was always locked. The room had a dim cloakroom with cubbyholes for coats and rubbers, and there was a tiny restroom in there with just a sink and a toilet. There were five or six low rectangular tables that held six children each, and the teacher had placed a big wooden block on each one, each block a different color, to identify the groups. We did most things with our color groups.

At the other end of the room was a wide fireplace, and before it a red circle laid into the tile floor. The whole class sat on the circle when Mrs. Coles read to us or we showed our toys at show and tell. We also laid mats down there when we napped. The teacher's desk was by the fireplace; behind it was a nook chock full of toys including a child-sized kitchen and a big gray wooden box with an old Ford steering wheel and column sticking out of it. Mrs. Coles was a stout, grandmotherly woman with sliver and white cat-eye glasses and white hair. She drove her gray 1968 Chevy Malibu coupe one whole block from her home to school every morning, where she parked on the street across from the school's east entrance. Curiously, she always sat in her car for five minutes fiddling with her purse before coming inside.

Clearly, my memory had switched on.

I often felt lonely in that room with 25 kids. I liked to drive the pretend Ford by myself, in part because I liked cars but also because it was safer not to risk playing with others. The boys pushed and shoved and chased each other and sometimes I got hurt. The girls never caused pain, but I didn't enjoy always being the husband or the son in their endless games of House.

Also, at a time when schools didn't teach reading until the first grade, I started Kindergarten already able to read. I was proud to be able to read, but Mrs. Coles didn't like it that I could. When I read her a page from a book, she seemed annoyed rather than pleased. I felt hurt that she wasn't as happy with my reading as I was. I also have a couple vague memories of her forcing me to write with my right hand, which confused and upset me because I was just as good with my left hand and liked writing with whichever hand was closest to the crayon.

I faced school as earnestly as I could, but I was lost. When my first report card came, the teacher had remarked in it, "Jimmy should smile more. He's so serious."

I'm not sure what changed in me. Maybe I wasn't quite emotionally ready for school. Perhaps something about my upbringing squashed my natural joy. Perhaps I was just depressed. Who knows; I can't reach those memories.

West Berlin, 1984

A clue came when I was 16. I spent a summer in Germany on an Indiana University exchange program where I would deepen my German language skills, which I had learned in three years of German classes. Even though my family always lived on a tight budget, my father stunned me by making the funds appear to send me on this trip. It took me a couple weeks to let my hair down and find my groove, but once I did I had the time of my life. I made some friends, lived with a nice family, studied German language and culture intensively, and traveled around Germany. I walked 539 steps to the top of the Cologne Cathedral. I drank beer in a little pub in Düsseldorf with a crusty but amused barkeep who explained the secret of the beer coaster and why you never turn it over. I got lost in West Berlin with a friend and spent an evening wandering streets to find our way back to our hostel. I touched the Wall and heard the stories of many who died trying to cross from east to west. I toured a prison where Nazi political enemies were hanged.

I stood on the ground where Christian writer Thomas a Kempis lived. I took a slow boat down the Rhine River and saw the Lorelei. I swam at a pool where clothing was optional from the waist up for everybody. I drank beer with East German teenagers and found that our differing political ideologies mattered not at all compared to our common desires for girlfriends, cars, and beer. It was heady stuff that produced a natural high, but also, I was given the freedom and trust to handle myself. It let more of the real me come out — and so joy returned. But when I came home, I experienced more than the natural letdown from such a wonderful trip — I found that the world to which I returned didn't fit the joyful Jim. Instead, it was shaped for the serious Jim. With sadness and resentment, I put joyful Jim away, and then the black curtain fell on my first major depression, which did not lift for months.

20 years or more ago popular psychology started talking about how everybody needs to get in touch with their inner child. Then as now, the idea makes me want to gag. But as I've worked through my issues over the years, joyous Jimmy kept appearing and asking for an audience to air his grievances for being put away for more than a quarter century. As I have listened to him, he has slowly been returning to his place within me. My, um, inner child is back! But I also find that the serious Jim isn't going anywhere. They are both parts of me. Maybe the inner-child crowd really means to say that without being all of who we are, which means bringing back all the parts of us we put away when we were little, we will always struggle to find wholeness, contentment, and peace.

The secret of the Düsseldorf beer coaster is that the bartender makes tick marks on the coaster for every beer you drink – and then flips the coaster over for the next drinker. If you flip it over, you might end up paying for however many beers the last person drank!

15 April 2007

Wanted by the FBI

On my flight to Germany in the summer of 1984, engine trouble forced us to land in Düsseldorf rather than in Frankfurt as planned. Because Düsseldorf expected no international flights that day, nobody was working in customs. My passport went unstamped, and I waltzed into Germany uncounted. How very un-German.

Several weeks later, my group visited Berlin. The Wall would not fall for five more years. At Checkpoint Alpha on the East German border, grave, armed border police in fitted olive uniforms boarded our bus and, without looking at or speaking to anyone, collected all of our passports, and exited. They made us wait more than an hour, our anxiety growing, before they returned with our passports all tossed into a box and waved us through. Each passport had received an East German stamp. The road from there to Berlin was bounded by walls so tall that we couldn't see over them even from our bus seats way up high. I guess the communists didn't want you to see the glorious living conditions on the inside, or everybody would want to move there. Several hours later down that road we were easily waved through the checkpoint at the West Berlin border.

A few days later we crossed into East Berlin to see the sights. At the famous Checkpoint Charlie, stone-faced border police once again boarded our bus, collected our passports, and made us wait for a long time before they returned them all stamped.

In East Berlin I walked in the Alexanderplatz, stood in line to buy a communist propaganda rag, er, newspaper (the top story that day was essentially how President Reagan was an idiot), drank beer and laughed with teenaged East Berliners, and tried to use a fetid underground open-pit public restroom. Shudder. I held it until we got back to the west.

At Checkpoint Charlie, 1984

In West Berlin, I bought a book called *Durchschaut die Uniform,* or *See Through the Uniform,* telling stories of border guards — not only about the distasteful jobs they did, but about the people they were. The last page showed two pictures of four border guards, the first with their stony faces and the second with wide smiles. The second photo seemed so strange! But I got the book's point, which was to have a heart because these guards were real people.

I decided to put on a pleasant face for them on the way home. As we left, we passed back through Checkpoint Alpha. Dour border police boarded our bus and collected passports. When they took mine, I looked them in the eye and smiled. It was met with indifference. They just took our passports and inspected our bus for things we were not allowed to take out. Inspection successful, they left and we were free to pass through. We made our way back across free Germany.

A few years later my passport was about to expire, and I renewed it.

I wondered if anybody at the passport agency noticed that my old passport contained stamps only from communist East Germany.

Then Iraq invaded Kuwait and the United States rode in on its white horse ostensibly to save the day. It was war, and I was draftable, so I was nervous about what might come.

At work the next day, my co-workers were subdued and serious. I worked as productively as I could while I listened to news reports on the radio. Midafternoon, the receptionist called from the main building. "Uh, Jim?" she said. I could hear concern in her voice. She paused. "Uh... Jim, there's a man from the FBI here to see you."

My mind reeled for several seconds. My passport! They must have a file with my name on it! They think I'm red! They've come to carry away the commies!

"Jim?"

"Um. Yes. Tell him to drive across the street to this building."

I stepped outside to await my doom. I paced under the gray sky, wondering what the internment camp would be like. Before long, a gray sedan turned in and parked. Out stepped a doughy man in a gray suit. He approached, showed me his ID, identified himself, and asked, "Are you James Grey?"

"Yes," I replied.

"Is there a place where we can talk privately?"

My brain screamed, "Talk privately? Aren't you here to purge the land of communists in the name of national security?" I was growing dizzy. I managed to mumble, "Sure, come inside." I led him to an empty room and we sat down.

"Mr. Grey, do you know a man named Robert Woolf?"

I've heard stories about what happens to cars that are accidentally shifted into reverse while going 40 miles per hour. Namely, the car's transmission suddenly disintegrates, distributing its pieces along the road. This is what happened to my brain at that moment.

In shock, I managed to say, "Yes, I know Bobby." Where the heck was this going?

"I need to ask you some questions about Mr. Woolf."

Bobby, a college friend and roommate, was a sharp, smart guy who majored in computer science and is now well-respected in his field. His senior year, as he looked for his first job, he applied at the National Security Agency. He was pretty jazzed about the job, but he never heard back from them. He applied for other jobs and eventually accepted one in Silicon Valley.

"Is this about the NSA job? Don't you know that Bobby accepted another position?"

The agent paused. He may have swallowed. He said, deliberately, "Yes, every person I talk to tells me that. But I have to do these interviews anyway."

So for twenty dull minutes he asked me questions about Bobby's associations and character. I told him what I knew and he went on his way. I felt sorry for the guy having to drive all over the place talking with Bobby's friends and family, needlessly looking for skeletons to qualify Bobby for a job he no longer wanted. I tried to empathize with the guy, but he'd have none of it. He stuck to his questions until he had no more to ask, and then he got back into his gray sedan and drove away.

I learned that it's fruitless to try to connect with a government official doing a distasteful or useless job. They just want to get it over with.

But at least there was no internment camp for me!

19 May 2007

On the small screen

I debuted on TV in 1976, back when stay-at-home moms were still called homemakers. There were enough of them then that locally produced homemaker shows aired in the morning on TV stations across the country. My hometown of South Bend was no exception, and WSBT-TV aired its homemaker show, *The Dorothy Frisk Show,* live each weekday morning right after *Captain Kangaroo.* The cloying strains of its theme music made my brother and I lunge at the TV to change the channel. We found *The Dorothy Frisk Show* considerably less exciting than staring at the wall and seriously less pleasant than eating Mom's liver and onions. But two young boys weren't in the target audience. Dorothy shared cooking tips, interviewed local notables, showed pictures of the newly born babies in town, and invited musical guests in to entertain the women at home.

My elementary school's choir was asked to sing Christmas carols on Dorothy's show one day that December, and another fellow and I were chosen to sing "Good King Wenceslaus" as a duet. I remember that Dorothy's set was in the same studio as the news set. That news set seemed vast on TV, but in real life it was incredibly small. I wondered how the anchors kept from getting in each other's way!

We assembled on our risers, the bright lights upon us. My buddy and I stepped forward for our duet. We wore simple costumes and mine included a brown cap that slid off my head just after we started singing. I kept my cool on the outside, but inside I was almost panicking. But then I felt the cap brush my left hand on the way down. I grasped it, gently placed it back on my head, and kept singing as if this were part of the act. I watched my partner's eyes grow wide when he saw it, but he kept singing, too. Even the choir director remarked about it in amazement afterward. My mom, who was along on the trip, was just proud of her son. I don't know anyone who actually saw me on TV that day!

Not a great photo of the WSBT building, but it's the only one I made

I didn't get to use any more of my 15 minutes of television fame until I was in college. I was General Manager of WMHD, the campus radio station. A reporter at a local TV station liked listening to us and wanted to showcase us. She and her photographer came out one afternoon and spent most of their time shooting records spinning on turntables and disk jockeys positioning the microphone. Then she interviewed me. I thought it was odd that she crouched on the floor, had me sit above her on the desk, and had the photographer shoot while he stood, but hey, she was the TV professional. I looked down at the reporter as we talked about the station's eclectic music, from bluegrass to Christian rock to death metal, all selected by the station's disc jockeys. I had been fairly serious during the interview but at the end I tried to lighten the mood by saying, jokingly, that we liked to "inflict our music on Terre Haute." Everybody in the room thought it was funny.

When the interview aired, the bad camera angle made it look like my eyes were closed. I also learned a valuable lesson that day: Don't say anything in front of a TV camera that you wouldn't want taken out of context. The way they edited the interview made it sound like we looked down on our college town and enjoyed making our station hard to listen to! The story came last in the newscast, and when it ended, anchors Gary and Marla were both laughing about it. Gary wouldn't let go of it, making several cracks as the closing theme ran and they faded to black.

There used to be a huge billboard on the edge of campus with Gary and Marla on it, confidently smiling down on US 40. Whenever I drove by it, I thought about climbing up there and painting their eyes closed!

27 July 2007

Adventures to come

I was excited for my sons on the days they started kindergarten. I left for work late so I could see them board the school bus. I could almost feel them growing up as they climbed the steps, their hands on the rail and their superhero backpacks hanging low. I'm sure my grin looked plenty goofy as I watched them go.

One son was absolutely thrilled to get to ride the bus. He had watched his stepbrother do it for years and was just sure it must be awesome and a real sign of being big. When I came home that afternoon, he chattered for a long time about the bus ride, telling me every detail. He mentioned that the school thing was okay too. His younger brother seemed unsure and nervous when his turn came, but because his bigger brother was there to show him the ropes, he did fine. I came home to find out he wasn't excited about school, though.

Somebody once told me that mothers always want their children to stay children just a little bit longer, while fathers are excited to watch their children to grow up. This seemed to hold true for my sons' mother and me. When the boys first boarded the bus, she mourned losing that bit of their littleness. I think she was like many other moms in that she also worried about the risks and dangers that could lie ahead. In contrast, I was excited because of the adventures and opportunities they would encounter. I love to see my sons reach new levels, whether it be learning to ride a bike, catching their first fish, starting middle school, or getting a driver's license. I want to see them become more independent so they can increasingly make their way in the world and experience life's goodness.

Still, I am glad for my sons as they are today. As I write this, my sons are playing in the living room as boys do, running around making laser and explosion sounds. I'm sure that one day I'll wish I could return to today, just for a little while, to hear them play again. But I'll be more than satisfied on that day if I can sit around the kitchen table with my grown sons, listening to stories of their adventures.

8 August 2007

Holiday lights along the Michigan Road

The Michigan Road is a historic road in Indiana, built in the 1830s to connect the Ohio River to Indianapolis to Lake Michigan. It was critical in opening northern Indiana to settlement. You can still drive the Michigan Road today, as a series of state and US highways.

After a nice Thanksgiving with my family in South Bend, I drove home Friday evening. I like to take the back way home along the Michigan Road, one of Indiana's oldest roads.

Downtown Logansport on the Michigan Road

This night I decided to shake things up a little and follow US 31 and then US 24 to reach the Michigan Road in Logansport. US 24 has been heavily rerouted across Indiana over the years. The new road is a four-lane slab, but the old two-lane road always winds along nearby. I meant to follow the slab to Logansport, but in the dark and drizzle I made a wrong turn and found myself on old US 24. I was ahead of schedule, so I decided to go along for the ride. The miles zipped pleasantly by.

Soon I entered Logansport in a part of town I'd never seen before. I passed through a retail district on the edge of town and then I entered a residential area. Trying to recognize landmarks in the dark, I made a turn onto what I thought was the Michigan Road, but that road ended two blocks later. I tried to find my way in stop-and-go traffic, something I had never seen in little Logansport. I soon found downtown, but no matter which way I turned, I found the streets closed. I kept backing up, turning around, driving a block, finding a barrier, backing up, turning around, and finding another barrier.

I spotted a police officer, so I got out of my car and explained my plight. "I'm just passing through and with all these barricades I'm pretty lost! I'm just trying to get to State Road 29." I knew that the Michigan Road became State Road 29 as it left Logansport. But because I'd paid no attention to local street names in any of the hundred times I'd driven through Logansport, I couldn't say which street I was looking for! He smiled at my story and opened the barrier so I could drive down the closed street. "Turn at 3rd St. That's 29." I passed through the opened barrier and was on my way.

As I drove out of town on the Dixie searching for a radio station, I happened upon one that was broadcasting live from downtown Logansport for the annual Light Up Logansport parade. That sure explained the traffic and the barricades! If I hadn't used up all of my extra time being lost in Logansport, I might have turned around to see!

No matter where I drive, I find more interesting things to see and do, more *life*, on the two-lane highway.

25 November 2007

Honoring my inner longhair

I chuckle at myself now as I share this story about, of all things, my hair, which I'd let grow to about my shoulder blades. I declare allegiance to my long hair – and then less than two years later I cut it off because I grew tired of caring for it.

When I was a teenager, I kept my hair very short. Mil spec. People sometimes asked if I was in ROTC.

Then in college I developed a used-record habit that Harold, my supplier at Headstone Friends music store, was happy to support. I skipped haircuts to buy more records. At first, when I'd go home on break Mom would hand me ten bucks and send me to the barber. She probably assumed I was broke and couldn't afford my own cuts. But soon Mom got wise to how I spent my money and stopped funding my haircuts. My hair grew out. When it started looking shaggy, people started asking when I was going to cut it. I had come to enjoy my hair, especially how it felt when it brushed against my skin. But the more people suggested it needed to be cut, the more I became determined to let it grow.

When my hair reached my shoulders, the handful of other long-haired men on campus started to acknowledge me. I had discovered the unspoken Longhaired Brotherhood, even though my hair was the shortest of the bunch and I didn't play electric guitar like they all did. One of the guys invited me to sing with his band. It turned out to be an audition, which I failed because the band's leader thought my rendition of Iron Maiden's "The Trooper" lacked guts. I got over it when, at a party, a lovely young woman couldn't keep her slender fingers out of my hair. We were an item for two years.

Yes, a mullet - it was the 80s after all

I dressed the part, with faded jeans and black concert T-shirts. I even got my ear pierced. My look brought challenges. Once when I was on the street, some scraggly shirtless guys in a rusty and dented old pickup truck slowed down, shouted out that I was a faggot, and then sped off. Another day I showed up at a new stylist's for a trim, her first appointment that day. The stylist wouldn't unlock the door for me until another stylist arrived. Turns out she was intimidated by my look and didn't want to be alone with me. She later felt bad, she said, because I turned out to be "such a nice guy." Then I worked a summer job for the state of Indiana, and our agency was being audited. The auditors had to pass behind me through my narrow office to get to their room. Every day, I heard the two women chattering happily in the hallway as they neared the office. When they entered, they very obviously hushed themselves, passed silently, shut their door, and then murmured about me – I could hear them through the wall. As they squeezed past on their last day, one of them stabbed her hands into my hair at the base of my neck. She exclaimed, "It's so clean!" I whirled around in surprise, but they moved on without looking at me.

As I neared graduation I had trouble finding a job. My long hair was absolutely not helping me land work, so I cut it off. I figured this was the cost of growing up. Years later, when the woman who would become my wife saw my old college photos, she excitedly asked me to grow it out again. Recognizing that one wife in a thousand would be this excited over long hair, I obliged her. In the winters I even grew a beard because she liked how rugged I looked. But by my early 30s, I felt like I looked more like Grizzly Adams than a heavy-metal god. And because I had become a family man and had ascended to management in my career, I thought that maybe it was unseemly to have long hair. So I went to a barber and walked out with a buzz cut. When I came home that night, my two-year-old son came into the living room to greet old Dad – and screamed! It was twenty minutes before he'd let me come near him.

After my divorce and as I pushed 40, the propriety of my 30s faded. I just wanted to do what made me happy, so I let my hair grow again. If this is my midlife crisis, I'm glad I chose this instead of a sports car or younger women. As my hair grew out, once again people commented about it. I was surprised that most told me it looked good, and only a few wrinkled their noses. Encouraged, I let it grow to my shoulders – long enough to feel good and frame my face.

While I first grew my hair mostly to thumb my nose at people and I next grew it mostly for my wife, this time I'm doing it purely because I enjoy it. I think that my inner longhair has always wanted to come out, but it's only as I pass into middle age that I can acknowledge him honestly.

I find greater acceptance today than 20 years ago. It probably helps that my hair's not quite long enough for me to be in the Brotherhood, that the heavy-metal T-shirts have been replaced with Oxfords and polos, and that many men wear earrings now – in both ears, even. The most backlash I get is the occasional woman who says, "I just couldn't date a man with long hair." And that's fine with me. My ideal mate's fingers will love spending time in there!

1 December 2007

Blizzard of '78

Thirty years ago yesterday the TV weatherman warned of a coming blizzard. By afternoon thirty years ago today, I sat in school watching a wall of white through the window as the storm moved in. School let out early. I leaned hard against the wicked cold winds, stinging snow against my face, as I walked the one block home. The snow froze to my eyelashes and my nostrils; I could barely see and had to breathe through my mouth. Dad wasn't home yet as the snow accumulated. He arrived hours late and on foot, crusted in ice and snow. He said his car got stuck somewhere down the street. He couldn't even tell if he was on the road.

The next morning, the radio said, "South Bend is shut down. Schools everywhere are closed." But the snow wasn't done falling. When it was stopped sometime the next day, 36 inches had fallen and had drifted as high as 10 feet. It was still dangerously cold outside.

Mom inventoried food while Dad tried to find a way out of the house. Every window and door was covered in drifted snow and would not open. With considerable effort he wrestled the garage door up to reveal a wall of snow that blocked the way but for a few inches at the top. Dad issued shovels to my brother and I and we started shoveling the dense, heavy snow into the garage. We worked in 20-minute shifts with long rests to get warm, and eventually dug a ramp up and out. Later we walked up that ramp and out onto the snow, dragging our Flexible Flyers behind us, to buy food at a nearby grocery that had opened somehow.

South Bend was paralyzed. People were stuck wherever they were when the storm hit. The same faces were on TV and voices were on the radio for days; they were all stuck at their stations. Nurses and doctors worked marathon shifts treating whoever could come in, which was good for my mother's friend who went into labor during the storm and was taken to the hospital by snowmobile. But at home the days dragged by with little to do but keep working on shoveling the driveway. A band of my braces broke; even though Dad cut the wire and packed it with wax, it still cut, and I suffered with it.

The city slowly began to clear the snow from the streets, making 10-foot piles at the curbs. People started to drive, though the streets felt like tunnels. The broadcasters and doctors got to go home. Dad found his car two blocks north in somebody's front yard, dug it out, and brought it home. We started clearing our sidewalks. Schools opened on a limited schedule two weeks after the storm. Dad was able to go back to work. I made it to the orthodontist.

The city started to function again, and so our normal lives slowly resumed in the coming weeks. Eventually, the mountains of snow melted enough that drivers could see what was around each corner. Schools returned to normal schedules. City services resumed. And one day the only remnants of the storm were tall snow piles in shopping-center parking lots. Even those eventually melted, but not until late April.

I still hate snow.

25 January 2008

Bursting the nostalgia bubble

In the first several years after I was newly single it was a great distraction from my troubles to spend a fair-weather Saturday seeing where an old road would take me. I still love the old roads today, and it's led to a broader interest in transportation history. I write about my road trips extensively on my blog.

My old friend Michael is an occasional companion when I take to the road. We took our first road trip together a few years ago along the National Road (US 40) in Illinois. The state built modern US 40 alongside an older brick and concrete road – and abandoned the old road.

My car on the old brick National Road right by Paul Ford's house

As we explored the abandoned road, Michael asked me what drew me to the old roads. I replied that it lets me enjoy imagining a time when drivers took it slow and enjoyed the scenery and people they encountered, something I wished for but found elusive. I said I wished I could hear stories about driving the old roads. Michael said, "I'll bet Paul Ford knows about this old road. He lives nearby. Want to meet him?"

Of course I wanted to meet him! Anybody who's ever worked in Terre Haute radio, as I have, knows Paul's name. He built Terre Haute's first FM radio station, WPFR, in 1962 and operated it through the early 1980s. Later, Paul started building a small network of Christian radio stations that he and his wife operate from their home on US 40 a few miles west of the Indiana state line and within sight of a strip of the old brick road. Michael volunteers at Paul's stations.

Paul dropped everything and sat down with us in his radio studio, which filled his house's front room. He was tickled to hear that I had worked for WBOW in Terre Haute because he had too, many years before. He told a ton of great radio stories, including getting his first radio job in high school, how hard it was to get advertisers on FM in the 1960s, and how he got to interview former President Truman in Indianapolis just after he left office by going to his hotel and asking. It was great talking with him.

I asked him about the brick road. "Oh yes," he said, "I used to drive on that when it was US 40 about the time my wife and I got married, which was in 1949. It was a dangerous road. People would get behind a truck, and they'd get impatient as it'd go slowly up the hills. They'd look for a chance to pass, but there were so many curves, and the road was so narrow. Eventually, they'd lose their patience and pass even if it wasn't safe. There were a lot of bad wrecks on that road."

I was a jarred by what he said. I thought I'd hear him talk glowingly of Sunday afternoon drives in the sunshine with his family, waving and smiling at people in oncoming cars, stopping at a farm stand for an apple. Instead, I felt the bubble of my idealizations burst. Pop.

As we drove away, I felt unsettled and wondered what made me enjoy following the old road so much if my nostalgic visions were false. But I started thinking of reasons pretty quickly. I enjoyed feeling connected to the National Road's history, following a path that had been in use for 170 years by generations of people making their way from eastern states into the Illinois prairies. I also enjoyed seeing the road's 1920s brick and concrete construction. I enjoyed knowing enough general road history to predict that the road probably wasn't even striped at first – because there were so few cars, people often drove up the middle and moved right when another car approached!

Michael on a rough patch of this abandoned road

But times changed in the postwar prosperity years during which Paul drove this road. Roads everywhere became more crowded as more people bought cars – for a time, demand for cars outpaced Detroit's ability to build them. Also, through the 1950s cars became faster and more powerful every year. The old roads' hills and curves just weren't engineered to handle so many cars going so fast. Paul's memory of the road made perfect sense. US 40 was soon rebuilt straight and wide, and later I-70 was built nearby with four lanes and limited access. Drivers could travel much faster and safer. They undoubtedly welcomed the new roads without looking back.

Reality certainly cast my nostalgia in the proper light. I realized that it represented something I very much want from life – a peaceful pace that lets me enjoy the journey. Even if the old roads never offered that to travelers in their day, they offer it to me now. On this trip, I got to spend most of the day with a longtime friend. We took it slow, averaging barely 20 miles an hour because of all our stops to explore. And I met someone interesting who taught me something new. Most of my old-road trips turn out this way. The very thing I imagined I missed, I can have today when I go out on the old roads.

8 February 2008

No fallow season

Wer rastet, rostet! – German saying
(Whoever rests, rusts!)

The Germans may be industrious, but we Americans are driven. Just before Christmas I read a Texas preacher's blog entry in which he reflected on how Americans like to push themselves past burnout and then spend a weekend on the couch in a stupor, recovering just enough to return to the burnout track on Monday. He linked to the post of a woman who, in contrast, had fled to Italy after a painful divorce, seeking to enjoy doing nothing as her path to recovery. She took a Sabbath to restore herself from depletion.

I left a comment that it must be nice to fly off to Europe to rest, but unfortunately after my divorce I have bills to pay and children to raise. But right then I was nearly tapped. Most days I was spent before the work day was done. After work, some nights I heated up an easy dinner, ran to whatever commitment I had that night, and sat there in a fog. The remaining nights I picked up my children, pushed myself to make dinner and do dishes, and then slumped into my recliner and stared blankly at the TV while my sons played or watched with me. I knew I needed to rest, but I was out of vacation time at work.

I had to do something, so I backed out of a standing Tuesday night commitment so I'd have one night a week at home alone. It didn't help. I found I needed to use my Tuesday nights to catch up on backed-up household work, and even then little home maintenance jobs were piling up. I still felt like I was running hard most of the time. I was on a project at work that frustrated me so much that I found it hard to get out of bed and make it to work. I turned to escape, staying up late watching TV or surfing the Net. Getting less sleep made things worse.

Then a few weeks ago I woke up one below-zero morning to find my bathroom pipes frozen. My kitchen pipes worked, so I shaved and brushed my teeth over the kitchen sink. As I tried to put my contact lens in, it blew away. I searched everywhere for it, including taking the pipes under the sink apart thinking perhaps it had gone down the drain. No luck; it was just gone.

I found my glasses – the prescription so out of date, they make me dizzy – and headed out to buy something that would thaw my pipes. At Menards, I slipped and fell on a patch of ice in the parking lot, breaking a rib. Then, in pain, I spent two hours under my house wrapping a heating element around my pipes. It didn't work, so I drove to Wal-Mart and bought an electric space heater and turned it on right by the frozen section of pipe. That worked in no time. But then I had to make an emergency appointment with an optometrist to get a new lens, which set me back $150. Meanwhile, I lost a day of work on that frustrating project, and its deadline wasn't relaxing on my account.

That day took all of the energy, patience, and good humor I had left. When I returned to work, I found my already thin patience with the project to be worn through. I kept to myself to avoid saying something I might regret, except for seeing my boss to tell her that when the project ended, I needed to take the two vacation days I had accumulated.

I took the days around a three-day holiday weekend for five days away. I thought I might catch up on my backlog of minor home repairs, clean the house thoroughly, bathe the dogs, do my taxes. But I lacked the energy and desire to work. I slept ten hours a night. I read. I napped. I binge-watched a DVD set of a favorite old TV program.

I did take a day trip. The dogs and I drove down to Madison on the Ohio River. I walked the dogs through Madison's early-1800s downtown, watching the people and enjoying the architecture. Then we followed the old Michigan Road, built in the 1830s, back home. Much of the route is a US highway today, but a couple long segments are just old country roads. We crossed two one-lane 1800s stone bridges on the route. The one in the photo seemed to be miles from anywhere. I hadn't encountered a car since I turned off the highway and wouldn't encounter another one until I rejoined the highway 20 miles later. The dogs were napping in the back of my little wagon, tired from their walk. I was alone on the old road, taking my time, enjoying the quiet. I could feel my heart beating in my chest just a little bit faster, as it does sometimes when I find joy.

The 1913 Shepard Bridge on the Michigan Road

Today is the last day of my five-day break. I've done a little house-work, and I went to see a movie, but otherwise I've relaxed and written this. I've regained some peace and I'm better rested. I think if I took another week off I could have my energy back, and if I took a month off I could have my spirit back. Since it will take months to save that kind of vacation time, there will be no fallow season for me. When I go back to work tomorrow, at least I won't be running on empty. But I want to keep it that way. I think I will plan a couple more long weekends in the spring, and a full week off this summer when my sons are here, as time to rest and take a couple short road trips just for the enjoyment. If I'm to rust, so be it.

19 February 2008

The Pintomobile

In the summer of 1986, I was home after my freshman year at engineering school when my Aunt Betty offered me a job driving for the courier service she owned. I told her that while I'd love to take the job, I didn't have a car to get there. She responded, "I have an old Ford Pinto that you can keep for the summer. I was going to have you drive it for deliveries most of the time anyway."

I loved this car beyond all reason

I drove that car all over northern Indiana and southwestern Michigan, running papers and small boxes to manufacturers. It was a great summer job, even though an old Pinto was neither a stylish nor, in this case, particularly reliable means of delivering anything.

The car's color masked a fair amount of surface rust, but color couldn't change the fact that most of the undercarriage was badly rusted. The floor pan had rusted through around two of the three bolts securing the front passenger's seat, but my girlfriend was kind enough not to complain about how her seat bobbed considerably at every bump.

Our biggest customer was AM General, which made military Hummers. (I know that the more common name for these is Humvee, but when AM General got the contract they called them Hummers, and that's what I'll always call them!) I got to ride in a Hummer a time or two, which was a big thrill. I delivered documents to their Mishawaka, South Bend and La Porte plants all the time. I liked the La Porte run because it involved a long, straight and fast stretch of State Road 2 the State Police seldom patrolled.

On one La Porte run, the whole back end of the car suddenly started shaking violently. Instantly, dust and rust bits filled the cabin. As I slowed down, the shaking diminished. As I pulled over, it became a rhythmic "whap" that was clearly coming from the right rear corner. It turns out that my frugal aunt had put retreaded tires on the Pinto, and the new tread had separated. Most of the tread on the right-rear tire was gone, and as it spun, the loose tread beat the crap out of the fender.

Fortunately, a good spare was stuffed in the uselessly tiny trunk, but when I cranked the jack into place against the car's frame, the metal crumbled away. I couldn't find a solid piece of frame anywhere so I could lift up that car. Thankfully, a previous driver had squeezed a bumper jack into the trunk and soon I was on my way.

The Pinto offered the La-Z-Boy driving position that was typical of several early 1970s cars: you leaned back deep in the seat, feet way out in front. It only served to magnify the Pinto's low-to-the-ground stance, and it seemed like most other cars towered over me. Despite being a small car, the Pinto was fitted with a giant steering wheel that rubbed my thighs no matter how I positioned my legs. Fortunately, the manual steering was light and easy once the car got rolling, and the wheel was easy enough to manage.

My Pinto had a 2.3-liter four-cylinder engine, a version of which ended up in the 1980s Thunderbird TurboCoupe. Mine must have been mistuned since it would accelerate right up to 30 mph from a dead stop without my touching the gas pedal. In sharp contrast to its overeager throttle, the Pinto's brakes were vague and unassisted, so stopping could be a real adventure. After running many just-turned-red lights because I couldn't get the Pinto stopped in time, I learned to take it slow in town and watch upcoming stoplights as far as I could see.

I also couldn't back up the car because its reverse gear had been stripped somewhere along the way. You'd think that would have taught me to always park so I could drive forward to get out, but I ended up pushing that car out of a parking spot about once a week. One client's office was on a hill, and twice – meaning I didn't learn the first time – I pulled into a space against their building only to have to push my car out later and then chase it down the hill. Have you ever caught a 2,000-pound car, rolling backwards and gathering speed, by an open door and tried to climb in?

Late that summer the car's cooling system failed. I carried water everywhere with me to top off the radiator until Betty finally put her in the shop for repair.

Really, this car was more hassle than it was worth; still, I loved it beyond all reason. It was the first car that was "mine" in that I didn't have to share it with my dad and my brother. It also was part and parcel of a job that gave me a tremendous amount of freedom. The Pinto and I explored the highways, stopped at the 7-11 for Big Gulps, listened to top-40 music on WLS, and soaked up sunshine all day. And I earned five bucks an hour doing it, which was great summer job money in 1986!

That's why even all these years later, I get excited when I see a Pinto that's still on the road. In idle moments I even occasionally troll eBay Motors' Pinto section. Maybe one day I'll find one in good nick.

30 May 2008

One-two punch

After five hours of hard rain during an unusually wet spring, a foot of water stood in my crawl space. I took the day off last Monday, borrowed a portable pump, and commenced Operation Dryout. It rained hard Tuesday and the crawl space filled with water again. Having learned much from Monday's soggy combat, I needed only Wednesday morning to retake the hill.

Back at work Wednesday afternoon, my co-worker said, "You look like you got a lot of sun," as I scratched at my cheek.

The back yard when I bought the house, ivy patch unkempt

An ivy patch surrounds my crawl-space opening. I didn't notice that it was laced with poison ivy. I was in it up to my elbows. Sloshing around under the house apparently saved my arms, but not before I touched my face. By Wednesday night my face was so swollen and tight that I couldn't pucker my lips to whistle. I wanted to scratch my bright-red cheeks off.

First thing Thursday I went to the doctor, who prescribed the usual one-two punch of steroid and antihistamine. I filled the scripts for methylprednisolone and hydroxyzine and took the first pills as soon as I got to work. They knocked out the itching and pain right now. But soon they started knocking me out, too. Unable to concentrate, I drove home. That turned out to be a poor choice – I've been better able to drive after drinking a six pack. I stumbled into the house, lay down, and passed out for five hours.

It turns out that hydroxyzine is known better as a sedative and tranquilizer than as an antihistamine. But it killed the itch better than Benadryl or Claritin, so I stuck with it through one more nap-filled day off work. Between the flooded crawl and the poison ivy, I worked maybe four hours last week.

Time for another one-two punch. I'm going to spray Roundup onto my ivy patch until every last green thing in there is dead. Then I'm going to get estimates to have a perimeter drain dug and sump pump installed in my crawl space. I know from experience that work doesn't come cheap – but it will be worth it.

16 June 2008

A place to start again

My home after 10 years of work to make it nice

Buying a house felt like the last step in reaching a new normal after my divorce. Looking forward to some permanence after three years of transience, I started looking at houses as soon as I was financially able. I wanted to live near my children, in their school district if I could.

We had made our home in the old northwest suburbs of Indianapolis. These homes had been a few miles outside the city limits until Indianapolis merged with the county in 1970. Lots are large, up to a half acre. The houses, mostly brick ranches, are set well apart. Most have attached two-car garages, but the cars that park outside do so under wide maples, oaks, ashes, and cottonwoods. Homeowners cut the grass on riding mowers and relax afterwards on their decks or in their patio enclosures. This was luxury suburban living for the 1950s middle class when they started to flee the city. The original owners did have to get used to hardships such as walking to the curb to get their mail, not watering their lawns lest they drain the well, and being careful of what they put down the drain so they didn't foul the septic tank. Even though most of these neighborhoods still lack city services, a strong school system keeps the homes in demand. To make it work, I was going to have to find a three-bedroom bargain, even in a depressed housing market.

On my budget, I kept seeing smaller homes that lacked at least one major feature, such as a second bathroom. Many of them would soon need major updating because they still had their original windows or the original furnace from 50 years ago. Several houses needed real work with fallen gutters, sagging floors, wet crawl spaces, and cracked ceilings. A few were basket cases, like the house with hardwood floors squishy from water damage, the odor of mold so strong that I got dizzy. Looking at these strange and sad cases, I felt like a gleaner picking over the harvested field.

After several months, I found a small brick ranch on a quarter-acre lot. It had been on the market for more than a year, probably because the furnace was 38 years old, the carpets were stained, the master bathroom was a fright, the kitchen lacked a dishwasher, and the third bedroom was teeny tiny. But the house was solidly built, the crawl space was dry, the family room had a fireplace, wood floors lurked under the carpets, a deck overlooked a wooded back yard that overlooked a golf course – and, most importantly, the price was right and it was less than a mile from my children.

I almost walked away because of the third bedroom. It was so small that I wasn't sure a twin bed would fit in it! But my brother suggested that if I gutted one of the room's two closets and turned it into an alcove for the bed, it would work.

So I bought the place. I went right to work on the bedroom. My brother helped me gut the tiny bedroom's closet, but I did the rest of the work alone, including repairing and mudding drywall, building shelves, painting, and tearing up carpet. I've never considered myself to be terribly handy around the house, but I pulled this project off very well, if I do say so myself.

While I worked on the bedroom, I started to assemble what I would need to live. I didn't get much furniture in the divorce settlement – a bright blue futon, my old mahogany dresser, and too many end tables. I bought everything else I needed on Craigslist, at Goodwill, and on clearance at Target. I carried all my purchases, including a dining room table and six chairs, home in my little station wagon. Some friends and a straight truck helped me move everything else.

I wrote last year about my first apartment and how I finished growing up while I lived there. I'm making a new start in my little house, and who knows how I'll grow while here. But already I have discovered that I'm far handier around the house than I ever thought I was, that I love my house being filled with my sons hoots and hollers as much as I love it when I'm all by myself reading quietly, and that there's great peace and pleasure in sitting on the deck with a cold drink while golfers hook their shots into my yard. I keep telling my boys we ought to sell the lost balls to pay for the inevitable broken windows!

20 June 2008

The world's foremost Jim Grey

I've had a small personal site on the Web since 1995. Those were the days when you wrote the HTML by hand in Notepad and then submitted the URL to Yahoo so others might find you. Yahoo ruled Internet search then, and I was the number one result when you searched on my name. The world has no shortage of Jim Greys; my name's pretty common. But it took a few years before any of the other Jim Greys had Web presences, and it was cool to be first. By the time Google had risen to search supremacy, a Canadian telephone company executive ruled the Jim Grey search. I swear his PR agency was paid by the press release. But that fellow appears to have retired, and so if you Google my name today, my homepage is the first hit. Once again, I am the world's foremost Jim Grey!

I've left quite an Internet trail, and you can find most of it via Google if you're patient. You will find an excerpt from a book about Microsoft PowerPoint I co-wrote several years ago, plus several places you can buy it if you're so inclined. You'll find most of the posts I made to USENET newsgroups in the early 1990s. And you'll find my profiles at LinkedIn, Facebook, and a few other places.

Be sure you don't confuse me with the non-me Jim Greys to whom Google also leads you. Just within the first hundred results, Google finds a Canadian ethanol executive, a ham radio operator, a Jewish man looking for love, an Oregon car and truck salesman, a chemical engineer hoping to find lost high school chums, and my dad looking for an argument. You'll also find *Jim Grey of Moonbah,* a children's book about an Australian boy who lived on a sheep ranch. I had that book when I was a kid.

But above all, beware the two impostors that Google finds who spell their last name wrong: Gray. The first is a highly regarded Microsoft researcher who sailed away in his boat last year and never came back. The second, a real scourge in my search results, is a sports reporter widely reviled for his abrasive interviews.

One little thing I didn't tell you is that I'm #1 only if you search for my name in quotes. If you leave off the quotes, the lost-at-sea Microsoft researcher's site pops to the top. I sure wish people could spell names right! Especially the hated sports reporter's name. Go check; people say things that would peel paint. You'd think they really hate me!

30 June 2008

Goodbye Rick, sort of

My brother and I didn't see eye to eye on most things when we were kids. We didn't hate each other, we just found each other to be extremely frustrating. We could make each other angry with very little effort. The house rule was that if we fought, whoever hit first was punished. I knew I had really pushed Rick's buttons when he pointed to his chin and said, "Hit me. Right there. Please."

Rick as a young teen

I was a year older, so I left for college first. After that I didn't see Rick except on holidays. He moved to my town eleven years ago, but I still saw him only on holidays. Our holiday times together were always fine, but somehow we seldom phoned and never dropped by.

But Rick was the first person I called when my now ex-wife wanted us to separate. He let me stay with him for a month, and he was a source of real strength as I started to recover from that horrible situation.

And then a couple years ago I ended up getting a job at the small software company where he worked. Understand that I'd spent my whole career, 17 years at the time, in software development. I even got my degree in mathematics and computer science, right up my career's alley. But Rick got a degree in psychology, then worked seven years as a preparator in an art museum and four processing mortgage loans before making another big career change into software. Both our careers had led to software quality assurance, his just through a very indirect route. We even reported to the same boss. And for the first time in our lives, my younger brother preceded me, and I lived in his shadow a little bit.

It has been great. Where daily childhood life emphasized our differences, adult work life has emphasized our similarities. We both like to think things through and do a thorough job. We both actively try to solve the problems we see. We both want to build team processes that make everybody more effective. We both want our teams' efforts to bring more value to the company. We regularly bounced ideas off each other, discussed thorny problems, and encouraged each other through challenges. I don't think either of us knew the other had it in him.

It has long been clear, though, that Rick has grown about as much as he can at our company and was losing his enthusiasm. He needed to learn new technologies and software development processes to get his fire back. And so when I come back from vacation a week from Monday his cubicle will be empty. He'll have a new job at a place that he thinks will provide the spark.

For the first time in my life, I'm going to miss my brother. Now that we have some momentum going, maybe we'll call each other sometimes.

31 July 2008

Eulogy for Buckethead

My stepson was over at a friend's house twelve years ago, running around in the back yard, when the Rottweiler next door sailed over the fence and bit him on the leg. The puncture wounds were not serious and they healed without complication. The dog's owner was mortified, apologized all over himself, and swore he'd keep his dog from clearing the fence again. We decided to let bygones be bygones.

Several months later my wife called me at work. "Jim, the people with the Rottweiler still feel so bad that they're giving us one of their new pups! Isn't that exciting?"

If the fact that they wanted to take the offending dog's progeny did not prove that my wife and stepson were completely mad, the fact that we had a five-month-old baby most certainly did. But as usual I buckled and we got the dog.

Worried about the Rottweiler reputation, overblown if you ask me, my stepson named her Sugar so all would know she was a sweet dog. But when my brother inexplicably nicknamed her Buckethead, it tickled me so improbably that it stuck.

Buckethead was on the small side, having been the runt of the litter, but she was smart, gentle, and obedient. My baby boy used to crawl up to her and yank on her ears, and all she would do was look up at me with long-suffering eyes until I intervened. She favored my wife and followed her around the house, which provided good opportunity for my wife to play "head bitch" (her words, not mine!) so Sugar would know the pecking order and her place in it. Sugar did challenge for top spot a couple times as Rottweilers will do, but my wife put her back in her place swiftly and efficiently. Her care gave Sugar lifelong contentment and happiness.

When my wife picked up a stray, abused dog, to our surprise Sugar took her under her wing and provided, in her doggie way, much of the same kind of esteem-building structure for Gracie that my wife had provided for Sugar. While Gracie will always have issues, I think Sugar's companionship gave Gracie a lot of security and kept her from being a basket case.

Our dogs' job was to secure the back yard against the great squirrel menace, and they poured all of their energy into it. When they spied one in the yard, they tore after it relentlessly, to the detriment of the patio enclosure's screens. One day, a squirrel trying to escape Sugar scaled the maple tree, and then Sugar made a flying leap and scrambled right up into the tree's crotch – which was six feet off the ground. She momentarily forgot about the squirrel as she looked down at the ground, her body's tension showing her puzzlement.

We had to coax her to jump down from the tree. After she did that, she realized she could go up there whenever she wanted to, and so she did. We used to entice her to do it to amuse our guests.

As she aged, arthritis crept into her joints, ending her tree-jumping days. And then my wife and I divorced. The dogs were hers, and she kept them; I didn't see either of them for a couple years. But nine months ago she asked me to take them, and what a blessing it has been to have them back! I enjoyed the quiet of living alone but missed having someone happy to see me when I came home. The dogs have been excellent company, and as the new top dog in their lives I've grown much closer to them. Sugar accepted the change with the characteristic good humor and serenity for which I always admired her, and set about making new routines in her new home. I wish Gracie had transitioned so easily! But Sugar was almost 11 years old, quite elderly for a Rottweiler. She lacked her old energy, and her arthritis had grown worse. Some days I couldn't get her interested in a squirrel in the back yard, and even when she did chase one, Gracie would sail off the edge of the deck after it while Sugar went down the steps gingerly before trotting out. I could see that I would have only so much more time with her.

Lately she has had some days where she lay around subdued, getting up only to eat and answer nature's call. Then yesterday her legs gave out underneath her twice while I got ready for work. The second time, she just crumpled into the grass and I had to carry her inside. The vet diagnosed autoimmune hemolytic anemia. He said that the treatment for it would be hard on her, especially at her age, and he estimated only a 30 percent chance of success. He said that without treatment, she'd die within a week – and it would be a horrible death by suffocation as her body destroyed her red blood cells. Yesterday I made the call that this was the end of the line for Buckethead. I scratched her ears and stroked her head until she was gone.

Everybody who's ever had a dog through its old age has a story to tell, and this one's mine. Gracie and I are both grieving in our way, but we will get along without old Buckethead. I'm telling people that to help Gracie cope with her big loss I'll be giving her extra attention and making some new routines – tonight, I put her on the leash and took her for a run while I rode my bike, something we've never done before. But the truth is these new routines will help me grieve and move on, too.

Goodbye, Buckethead! You were an excellent dog.

15 August 2008

Monopoly money

I was feeling good about my financial situation as I headed into the summer. I was rapidly paying down debt and had built up some savings. But then August was unexpectedly expensive. I replaced my car's transmission (and rented a car for two weeks while it was in the shop), replaced my refrigerator when it conked out, and had some medical and veterinary bills. Bam! Within a few weeks, my savings was gone and I had even gone a little more into debt.

I know that everything that cost me was just a matter of chance. Cars break down, 20-year-old fridges die, dogs and people get sick. It was better to spend savings on these things than to have borrowed to pay for it all. You might even say that God took care of me, providing for me through these misfortunes. But I've been angry about it just the same. It really hurt to get a little bit ahead only to lose it almost all at once.

On Wednesday, the boys and I broke out the Monopoly board. My youngest is starting to understand trading and can now stick with a long game, and so our play is starting to become vigorous. We'd made some trades and we all had monopolies — my older son had the violets, my youngest son had the neighboring oranges, and I was just around the corner with the reds. When we started improving our properties, it became hard to move along that side of the board without somebody collecting.

My youngest son landed on my Kentucky Avenue. With two houses, the rent wasn't terrible, but having spent all his cash on houses he hocked most of his property to pay me. He weathered that with good humor, but he next landed on Go To Jail and so would make another trip down Death Row. His next roll put him on Community Chest, but then he landed on Indiana Avenue, which by then had four houses and was much more expensive to visit. Cash-strapped and hocked to the hilt, he had no choice but to sell most of his houses. He was ticked. And then a few tears ran down his face. And then he buried his face in my shoulder.

The irony did not escape me as I hugged him and told him it's bound to hurt when you build things up and get a little ahead only to have bad luck take it all away.

When I woke up the next morning, *I* didn't feel so bad anymore.

30 August 2008

Summer's denouement

During my 1970s kidhood when schools started after Labor Day as God intended, my mid-August birthday always meant summer was beginning to end. By then, the afternoon sun was at its hottest and most intense, the annual August dry spell began to toughen and dry all that had been green, and the street lights switched on earlier to send everyone inside for long quiet evenings with our families and our TVs.

The dozens of children all up and down Rabbit Hill, as our parents nicknamed our prolific neighborhood, always sensed these changes. We squeezed in as much play as we could before time ran out. One fellow down the street, thinking he was Mickey Rooney in Babes in Arms, always organized and directed an end-of-summer show, an extravaganza that nobody would come and watch because everybody was in it. I would push to reach the new tree-climbing heights my brother and his best friend had mastered weeks before, heightening their schadenfreude when I would inevitably fall, have the wind knocked out of me, and make that loud but hilarious sucking noise that only sounds like death is imminent. Somebody would connive their mother into have a big running-through-the-sprinkler get-together at which gallons of Kool-Aid were served. Several kids sold lemonade or toys at a family garage sale to raise money for Jerry's Kids. The chubby fellow who lived where the street curved sang his slightly naughty rhymes more often ("In 1944/My father went to the war/He stepped on the gas/And blew out his ass/In 1944!"). And then the Jerry Lewis telethon was on everybody's TV. It was Labor Day weekend, and we all knew it was over.

Blurry photo of Christy and Brian, who staged the annual summer show, in front of the house I lived in

On the day after school started, we could still play war in full army gear in the wide easement behind the houses, ride our bikes and Big Wheels up and down the hill making siren sounds as if we were a horde of ambulances and police cars (imagine 20 children doing this on your street!), play endless Red Rover in the freckled girl's front yard, and watch the four-year-old girl next door eat sand with a spoon (oh, if her mom only knew). But we didn't, hardly. We lost our enthusiasm. It was time to button ourselves back down and return to school-day routines.

Rabbit Hill conditioned me well; I still recognize and lament the signs of summer's end. Kids have been back in school for weeks already. The grass hasn't grown much lately because of the annual dry spell. My air conditioner has been off more days than it's been on; it was too chilly the other morning to drive to work with the window down. I've crammed as much outside time as I can into these days to enjoy their freedom, but the end is in sight. Shorts will soon give way to long pants and short sleeves will give way to long sleeves. I'll be in a windbreaker with a rake in my hands, collecting my trees' deposits. The snow will fly and I'll be hunkered down at home.

I still feel restricted, buttoned down, in fall and winter. Here's hoping for a long, warm Indian summer first!

14 September 2008

Headstone's

When I was in college, I should have just had my work-study paycheck direct-deposited into Headstone Friends' bank account. I spent most of it there anyway on used records and CDs.

Headstone's is a music store in head-shop trappings. Step inside, and suddenly it's 1969. Well, it's 1969 after your eyes adjust to the dim light. But you smell the sweet incense right away and hear the loud music from the parking lot. The counter is on the left, offering cheap jewelry and silly buttons and, at least at one time, scales and rolling papers. On the right are ceramic dragons and fabric Led Zeppelin and Jimi Hendrix wall hangings and a rack of incense sticks. Then racks of CDs line the wall all the way to the back where a few bins of records remain. In the corner, next to the drinking fountain that has never worked, is a room aglow with black-light posters.

Things do change at Headstone's. When I first set foot in the place in the 80s it was half the size it is now, full of waist-high record bins. They expanded into the building's back section a few years later, and slowly tall homemade CD racks crowded out most of the record bins. And every so many years, when the building's mural and sign are faded and worn almost beyond recognition, they repaint. When I was there last Saturday, it looked pretty fresh.

Headstone's is seriously old school. They have one location, at Poplar and 12th Streets in Terre Haute. They're not on the Web. They don't take credit cards. The owners, aging hippies who were about the same age I am now when I first visited, work the counter. They keep inventory records on index cards in cardboard boxes. When you find a CD you want, you go to the counter and have someone come unlock the cabinet for you. Then they total your purchases on paper receipts and calculate the tax by hand.

The staff is very low key, but while I lived in Terre Haute I visited so often that they came to recognize me. One fellow named Harold became friendly and came to recognize my buying habits. One day a college friend came by my dorm room and said that I should see Harold next time I was in. He had set aside a promotional poster from a Paul McCartney album for me. The album wasn't Paul's best, but the the cover photo, of Paul and his wife taken with the kind of camera used for 1940s Hollywood glamor shots, was outstanding, and larger than life on the poster. "We get this junk all the time and never use it," he said. "You buy all kinds of Beatles and McCartney so I figured you'd like to have it." Sure enough! I had it framed. Despite generous offers from collectors, it still hangs in my house.

Harold was there on Saturday. I haven't seen him in at least ten years, but he looked just the same – long brown-and-gray hair curling halfway down his back, reading glasses at the end of his nose, and a round, tan fisherman's hat covering his head. There was a glimmer of recognition on his face when he saw me, but it had been so long I wasn't sure he'd remember me even if I did give him my name, so I kept to myself. I didn't find any CDs I couldn't live without, but just for fun I did buy a tie-dyed T-shirt. It filled my car with Headstone's scent all the way home. I hated to wash it.

22 October 2008

On the Dummy Line

What fun songs do you remember singing as a child?

I read a blog post this morning quoted a line from an old song about trains that I learned in the second grade but haven't thought about in years. The teacher gathered our class around the piano every day and we sang songs from a set of discarded songbooks that had been part of the curriculum many years before. The book included this song, which we sang often – because I liked it and asked for it all the time! I still remember my favorite verse and the chorus:

> Got on the Dummy, didn't have my fare
> Conductor said, "What'cha doin' there?"
> I jumped up and made for the door
> And he cracked me on the head with a two-by-four!
> On the Dummy, on the Dummy Line
> Rise and shine
> Rise and shine and pay your fine
> When you're riding on the Dummy, on the Dummy Dummy Line!

I Googled it and found that there are many songs about trains with "dummy" in the title, including this one. Turns out that this is a folk song with roots going back as far as the 1890s. It's about hoboing on the railways on "dummy trains," the trains being "dumb," meaning quiet, because they used locomotives with condensing engines that eliminated the noise of steam escaping. Other versions involve trolleys or short branch railways, the cars pulled by small steam engines that sometimes were "dummied up" to look like passenger cars so the sight of them didn't frighten horses on city streets. I gather that this kind of dummy train was known for being slow, reflected in this lyric I found but don't remember:

I said to the brakeman, "Can't you speed up a bit?"
Said he, "You can walk, if you don't like it"
Said I, "Old man, I'd take your dare
But the folks don't expect me till the train gets there."

I wouldn't have cared about any of this when I was in the second grade. I just got a big kick out of singing about that poor guy getting hit on the head with a board!

12 December 2008

Photographic holiday memories

My grandparents always owned the latest Polaroid cameras, and they passed on that tradition in 1977 when they bought my brother and me Polaroid Super Shooter cameras for Christmas.

When I unwrapped the gift, I remember thinking how cool the box was. I liked the box so much that I kept my camera in it for the almost 30 years I owned it. Not long ago I learned that the box, like all Polaroid packaging of the day, was designed by Paul Giambarba, a top designer who was a pioneer of clean, strong brand identity.

I remember how easy it was to spot Polaroid film on the drug store shelf because it had the same rainbow-stripes design elements as the camera's box. Film and developing for my garage-sale Brownie cost about half what a pack of Polaroid film cost, but the colorful Polaroid boxes on the shelf always tempted me. I often decided that next time I bought film, I would save my allowance for the whole month it took to afford a pack of Polaroid.

My brother also got a guitar that Christmas morning. My new camera came with a pack of film, so I loaded it and shot a photo of him on his first day with his guitar. He played that guitar for 20 years! He looked strange as an adult playing a kid-sized guitar!

20 Christmas Days later, when my older son was not yet a full year old, my wife gave my brother her old guitar. Our boy, drawn to the music, wouldn't leave his uncle's side as he played that evening. Steadying himself on his uncle's knee, he looked up with wide amazement in his eyes.

May this holiday bring you the gift of excellent memories to share with your loved ones down the road.

22 December 2008

Essays

It's cliche to say that I write to figure out what I think, but it's true. Many times as I've turned over thoughts in my head about a topic and couldn't decide what my position was. Writing it out always clears it up, even though it is real, hard work, because it forces me to think the topic through.

In contrast, sometimes I have a point to make and I write a story that illustrates it.

You'll find both kinds of essays here.

Pride of workmanship, part 1

Me on the air at WMHD, 1987

Quality guru W. Edwards Deming, who helped transform Japan into an industrial powerhouse, claimed that workers who feel pride in the quality of their work are critical to a company's success. Pride in my work is certainly critical to my satisfaction on the job, right along with being challenged and enjoying the environment. When I have those three elements, I love my job.

I am fortunate to have lived one of my dreams. Ever since I was a boy, I wanted to be the voice coming out of the radio. In college I got my chance at WMHD, the campus station. Not only did I get to speak on the air, but I also got to play whatever music I wanted. It was a lot of fun. I figured out how to match key and tempo to make one song flow well into the next. We had few CDs, which were new then. So I learned to slipcue and crossfade vinyl on our two classic DJ turntables, which let me create coherent mosaics of music across each two-hour shift. I also developed an on-air voice that I thought sounded smooth and professional. My peers at WMHD liked what I did, too, because one year they named me "DJ of the Year." Today, I still listen to tapes I made of some of my WMHD shows, and they always make me feel good.

After I graduated, one day I was out at an event in town and I happened to be wearing an old WMHD T-shirt. Local radio station WBOW was there, promoting the event. WBOW was what they used to call a "full service" station, with news, community events, music from my grandmother's era, and on-air "personalities" to bring it all together in an entertaining way. One of those personalities was at the event that sunny afternoon, a solidly-built man with the darkest red hair I'd ever seen. He approached me, introduced himself as Chip, and asked if I worked in radio. I told him about WMHD, and he asked me if I'd be interested in part-time work at his station.

A couple weeks later, I was very excited to be sitting at the controls in WBOW's studio. Chip was there to show me the ropes. He explained the format clock' showed me how to find songs, jingles, sweepers, and spots in the cart library; showed me the liner cards; and said that I needed to backtime to the news at the top of the hour. Clock? Spots? Jingles? Sweepers? Cart? Liner? Backtime? It was a whole new language. Except for opening the mic and talking, WBOW was unlike anything I'd ever done on the radio. I was in over my head! As Chip figured out how little I knew, he rolled his eyes, sighed, muttered something about how hard it was to find experienced talent in "this nowhere market," and began to teach me about professional radio.

It took me weeks to understand the clock so I could do a smooth break, and months to get good at backtiming the last 15 minutes of every hour so the last thing I played ended just as news from the ABC network started at precisely the top of the hour. Every week, I recorded a cassette of my show — just the parts where I talked, which Chip called a "scoped aircheck" — and Chip and I reviewed it together. As we listened each week, he bluntly challenged me to get better. "Stop saying degrees! The high tomorrow will be 58! Everybody knows that's 58 degrees! And right there, you did that *annnd* thing again as you moved from one topic to another, like you're connecting cars on a train. Cut it out! I want to hear you go smoothly from the beginning of your break to the end! And you stepped on the vocals on that song! C'mon, time it out, know what you're going to say and how long it will take!" Chip did not pull punches.

I sometimes came by the station during Chip's shifts and watched and listened to how he did things. He thoughtfully prepared for every break, reviewing material he brought in with him that day to talk about. Before he opened the mic, he made sure everything he was going to use — a liner card, maybe a newspaper clipping, and all the spots (commercials) — were ready to go. Then he put his hands on the buttons and knobs he would use during the break and sat quietly under his headphones, listening to the end of the song that was playing. He knew how every song in the library ended, and he would count beats as he opened the mic so he could start talking at just the right moment. He had a subtle sense of timing — he always knew the very moment, a sweet spot in time, to do the next thing, and how to do it in a way that kept the audience's attention. I could see he was doing what he was trying to get me to do, and I started to hear how these little things were the difference between some guy playing music and talking, and a talented pro delivering fresh, vital radio that kept listeners tuned in because they wanted to hear what was next.

As I kept practicing on my weekend shifts, it started to click. I could hear myself getting better on my aircheck tapes. I looked forward to Chip's weekly beatings, as he called them, because I'd always take away something new to work on. I realized I was learning from somebody who knew his stuff, and that such opportunities were rare in markets as small as Terre Haute. Later, I learned that opportunities to learn from someone who really knows his stuff are rare in *life*. When Chip started reviewing my airchecks monthly rather than weekly, I realized with satisfaction that I had achieved basic mastery, and that I was starting to sound like a pro.

Because Chip vigorously coached the whole on-air team, WBOW sounded better than you'd expect in a small town like Terre Haute. We all took pride in how tight we sounded. We could have been more competitive if we could have played more contemporary music, but Chip couldn't convince the station's owner of it. Eventually the owner decided he could make as much money by replacing all of us with a satellite programming service. This was the fate of full-service AM radio across the country and today the format no longer survives. Neither did the WBOW air staff. Chip was the first to go, and I left shortly after. The rest of the staff was laid off in time. The solid on-air work Chip brought out in the entire team, and the high-quality service we provided as a result, was not enough to overcome financial reality. I still struggle with this lesson. But I am still proud to say I was part of WBOW.

4 June 2007

Pride of workmanship, part 2

I moved to Indianapolis many years ago to take a job editing technology books. My first project was editing a new edition of one of the publisher's biggest sellers. I drew this plum assignment not for my l33t editorial sk1llz, but for being the new guy. You see, the author had a reputation for running his editors ragged, and nobody wanted to work with him. They were glad to scrape his book onto me.

I never understood why. Editing the author's work was a pleasure – his writing was clear, engaging, and funny. When I made suggestions for improvement, he gladly took most of them. He even called me to discuss and improve on a few of them. He did require a lot of attention, all of it for the good of his book, as he sweated every detail. For example, I spent hours on the phone with him poring over proofs, which are draft printouts of the book after it's been laid out. It's the last stage before the book is printed. At this late stage, he sometimes rewrote entire paragraphs to make them funnier or reworked graphics to make them clearer, all of which never ceased to thrill the overworked layout department.

When we were done, we had a book to be proud of. After the book was printed, I displayed my copy prominently on my bookshelf. It then sold a bazillion copies.

Then I got my next assignment, a thick book about a communications technology still popular then. This author handed in cumbersome and clumsy text full of basic writing errors. His lame humor was often offensive. His technical explanations were usually incorrect and incomplete. I spent hours hammering his work into something marginally usable. He then ignored half of my queries and barely responded to the other half.

After he had handed in 100 of the book's 800 pages, he announced that he was done writing. I was incredulous as he explained that the rest of the book would be documentation from shareware related to this technology. He wanted to publish 700 pages of shareware documentation he didn't even write! I accosted the acquisitions editor – that's the guy who hired this author – and raised an unholy ruckus. I said, "This book will be useful to nobody!" He shrugged. "It's his book. Is it on schedule?"

I spent the next several weeks with my stomach knotted from anger and disgust as I formatted and edited those 700 pages. I pinched my nostrils shut as I sent the chapters to layout. I suppressed my gag reflex as I reviewed the proofs. I rolled my eyes when my copy of the finished book arrived. I hid it in a dusty and forgotten corner of my bookshelf. Then I succeeded for several weeks at forgetting the whole sordid ordeal until I received a letter from somebody who actually bought the book. He wrote something that knocked me out of my chair:

"Dear Sir. I was trying to break into this communications technology when I found your book. I wanted to tell you that it was exactly what I needed. I played with a couple of the programs the book described and, with the book's help, got one of them running. Thank you for publishing this book. Sincerely, Some Reader."

I was humbled. No, I was shamed. Mr. High-and-Mighty Editor thought that the author created a steaming pile of feces while giggling at the teller's window as he signed his advance check. Yet somebody found the book to be exactly what he needed.

I started to see that maybe I wasn't the final arbiter of quality, that maybe quality is what meets the customer's needs. I've carried this critical lesson into every job I've had since.

But now, 13 years later, I have learned another lesson from these two books.

That first book was *Macs For Dummies, Third Edition*, by David Pogue, a keystone of the For Dummies franchise, which was huge then. More recently, you might have seen David's technology column in The New York Times, or his acclaimed "The Missing Manual" series of books, or maybe the occasional stories he does for *CBS News Sunday Morning*. David has done very well for himself since his Dummies days. It helps that David is charismatic and gracious in person, has a knack for leveraging opportunity, and sells himself hard and well. I think that David's drive and ability to do top-flight work gives him something solid to sell that distinguishes him from someone who just schmoozes glibly.

I haven't been very kind to the other author here so I won't reveal his name or the title of his book, which did not sell well despite the one fan letter. I found his home page on the Web this morning and he seems happy. But he has not achieved a hundredth of what David Pogue has.

The new lesson? Something modest may meet a customer's need. But it sure is satisfying – and the hard work sure worth it – when you can really delight the customer. And David Pogue's case shows that talent and hard work can still really pay off.

23 June 2007

What's the use?

In 1989 I bought my first brand-new car. I'd been driving a car that belonged to my dad. But I had just graduated college, gotten a job, and moved into an apartment. Dad said, "Enough freeloading; I'm coming in two weeks to get my car back." I looked for a used car, hoping to save money, but nobody in town would lend me money because I had no credit history.

Disappointed but undaunted, I turned to General Motors, which offered to lend me up to thirty thousand dollars to buy a new car. "You've achieved so much," the form letter said, "with your recent graduation. We think that makes you a good risk, so we invite you to reward yourself with a fine new General Motors car." I went to a Chevy dealer and, resisting considerable upselling, picked out an entry-level car, a maroon coupe with four cylinders and five speeds. I splurged on a cassette stereo; everything else was as basic as I could get. The interest rate was obscene, but I could manage the payment, so I signed the loan papers on a Thursday. Besides, Dad was coming on Saturday whether I had a car or not. With just 16 miles on the odometer, I drove it home.

I'd never driven a new car. It cruised so smoothly! It passed without sounding like it would rattle apart! That stereo really rocked! Still, I was not enjoying the car payment, and realized that I would want to keep this car long after it was paid off. This meant keeping my car in top shape so it would be worth having then. So I followed the maintenance schedule religiously and had even small problems checked out. I also washed and waxed my car about every week and kept the interior clean, because I'd want it to look good in the future, too.

And then the troubles started.

One week after I bought the car, the drive thru at McDonald's didn't put the lid tight enough on the orange juice, and it spilled everywhere. I never got it fully out of the seat, the door fabric, and the carpet.

After about a month, a dying tree hanging over the road decided to deposit one of its large branches on my car's roof as I drove under it. Just after I got the car back from the body shop, an F-350 with an iron flatbed decided to change lanes without checking his mirrors. It did $2,000 worth of damage.

Nobody told me that in an accident I should get a police report and that I should then call the other fellow's insurance company to open a claim. No, I opened the claim with my insurance company. On top of paying my deductible to repair this damage, my insurance company charged me a special fee of several hundred dollars as they believed I had caused the accident. I didn't know they could do that! They also nearly doubled my rate, which was already terribly high because I was male, unmarried, and under 25. I changed insurance companies, which brought my rate back down. But I still had to eat peanut butter and hot dogs for three months while I recovered from that financial mess. And then the body shop screwed up the repair so badly I had to take it back three times for fixes.

Then the windshield wipers quit working, and it took the dealer three tries to get the repair to last. After about eighteen months, the stereo died. I saved up and put a new one in myself. Then the power steering pump started making strange noises. It took the repair shop four tries to put in a pump that worked.

I'd had the car about four years when I was hit in the right rear corner after I hit a patch of ice and slid partway off the road. What looked like minor body damage turned out to be several thousand dollars worth of frame straightening. The body shop did a pretty good job, but still the front-seat passenger could pretty easily put their foot on a particular spot on the floor and with very little pressure make it pop like the lid of a baby-food jar.

Then one day when I tried to turn the car off, something snapped and my key spun freely in the ignition. Turns out that a long aluminum rod broke in half, one that connected the key to the starter. The mechanic had to remove the steering wheel and disassemble the steering column to replace it. When he reassembled everything, the steering wheel wasn't straight. When I insisted they get that right, they sent their burliest mechanic to try to intimidate me into leaving. When that didn't work, they got it on straight all right – by breaking the steering column. I could move the steering wheel about an inch up and down or left and right. I was disgusted, but not wanting to deal with those mechanics anymore I drove it away like that. I ended up never getting it fixed. The car drove fine.

After about six years, the headliner started coming down over the back-seat passengers' heads. I reattached it with neat rows of staples. I noticed that the clear coat was chipping off both doors. And finally, one day as I leaned back to square my butt in the seat, a bracket that held the seat to the floor sheared in half, the seat fell back, and I found myself suddenly staring at the neat rows of staples in the ceiling. Thankfully, I hadn't started the car yet. I fixed that myself with a bracket from a junked car like mine.

The last couple years I owned the car I washed it maybe once a year, and I'd let it go long between oil changes. My enthusiasm for the car was gone. I believed I had wasted my effort to keep the car nice, and I felt a lot of disappointment. What was the use when outside events had conspired against my little car so much? I didn't expect it to last forever, but I had wanted it to stay nice longer. And then, as if in defiance during those neglectful years, it lasted 150,000 miles and showed no signs of stopping when I sold it. For a late-1980s Chevrolet, that was a very long life.

Cars fall apart, of course. It's what they do. I was naive to think my car would stay like new for so many years. But to my surprise, now that ten years have passed since I sold that car, I look at it differently.

I remember the day I found a long, straight stretch of deserted highway and put my foot to the floor. With a big smile on my face, I learned that my car could go just beyond 100 miles per hour.

I remember how well it held the road when I pushed it through curves and over hills. I could get it momentarily airborne on a rise around a particular curve on a little-traveled back highway. I hope it's not too indelicate to say that my car's handling made my butt happy.

I remember long road trips I took in my car – a sweep through Detroit, Toronto, Niagara Falls, and Hoboken by myself to see old friends, and a trip to the Kanawha Valley of West Virginia with my dad to see where he grew up and meet relatives I never knew I had.

I remember listening to mix tapes in my car as I drove around town. I often sang along, not caring whether anybody else saw me.

I remember driving in my car to the old mill dam in Terre Haute with my girlfriend, where we'd sit and talk to solve world problems, and maybe have a smooch.

I remember my soon-to-be wife getting me out of a speeding ticket in my car.

I remember a frigid January day when I brought my first baby home in my car.

In other words, I remember *enjoying* my car as it took me places and helped me spend time with people I loved.

It's easy to think that I feel better about the car now because time heals all wounds. But rather I think I was so focused on making the car last that I was often closed to enjoying the car while it lasted.

I've been studying the book of Ecclesiastes lately. The last part of chapter 2 talks about the frustration of working hard to build up something only to later have to hand it over to somebody else, who may screw it all up. Even though this isn't exactly my car story, verses 22-25 do apply:

> What does a man get for all the toil and anxious striving with which he labors under the sun? All his days his work is pain and grief; even at night his mind does not rest. This too is meaningless. A man can do nothing

better than to eat and drink and find satisfaction in his work. This too, I see, is from the hand of God, for without him, who can eat or find enjoyment?

I spent a lot of time chasing after the wind, as Ecclesiastes says, on my car. There was nothing wrong with taking care of my car – it is prudent to take care of our things so they last as long as they can. But my taking care of it interfered with my ability to experience the joys of owning and using it. I didn't even enjoy washing and waxing the car; I did it mostly from my drive to keep it nice. It was like I was compulsively hoarding pennies in a jar for another day, checking my jar every day to see how many pennies I had, hoping that I could count on those pennies in the clutch. I wasn't living in the present, enjoying everything I had in that moment.

Today I drive a red Toyota hatchback. It had been my ex-wife's car and she had picked it out, but when we split she wanted our family car instead. I wish it were a color other than red and I wish it had a little more power. But little car has grown on me anyway. I love its fuel economy, its CD stereo, and that the hatch can swallow a huge amount of stuff. I don't have as much time as I used to for washing and waxing my cars, but I took this photo right after I managed to put a good shine on her.

This car is not without its troubles. The clutch makes a bad noise when it's humid or damp outside, the car sometimes stalls when just starting to roll, I've has lost five wheel covers so far at $80 each, and I'm about to have to take the car back for the fourth time to get a brake job done right.

I hope I can simply enjoy this car as I drive my boys to the park in it, take it on road trips, drive to work while singing along to my music, make trips to visit friends in other states, and yes, wash it and wax it and keep to the maintenance schedule so it will last.

6 July 2007

Shopping in the suburbs

I've always lived in cities. I groove on grids of streets with curbs and sidewalks. When I moved to Indianapolis, I didn't consider for a minute living in the suburbs – the bedroom communities that ring Indianapolis.

But to get a better school system, I did buy a home outside the traditional part of the city with its grid of streets. My early-suburban home was in a maze of cul-de-sac neighborhoods that even now lack certain city services such as water, sewer, and snow removal. These neighborhoods empty onto large arteries, which connect with larger arteries, which pave the way to large, generic shopping strips.

Money is tight so I shop Walmart, which is about 20 minutes away along congested roads. It's always packed, and I have to park at the back of the lot. Customers are rude. The unhelpful staff all have thousand-yard stares. The checkout lines have ten full carts in them.

And then I have to drive back along those congested roads. I always come home whipped.

The other day, a lady at church said that she goes to the Walmart in Brownsburg, a nearby suburb. She said it might take a few extra minutes to get there, but its a much nicer store. So yesterday I made my grocery list and headed out to try it.

I've traveled the two-lane road to Brownsburg many times to visit friends. Traffic is usually light, making for a pleasant drive past a lush city park and over a reservoir, and then into the next county with cornfields and new housing developments. I enjoyed this trip as I always do -- and arrived a full five minutes faster than I could ever get to my usual Walmart.

I parked about mid-lot. As I navigated the store, I heard something I had never before heard in Wal-Mart: politeness from fellow shoppers as we steered our carts around each other. "Oh, pardon me." "Excuse me." "Oh, I'm sorry!" I quit counting after the tenth apology, and by the time I was ready to check out, I caught myself thinking that it was becoming tedious to return so many apologies!

Except for those polite exchanges, and the normal-volume conversations of other customers, the store was remarkably quiet. Even though I had to go back and forth through the store's unfamiliar layout to find everything I wanted, I felt none of the usual tension or fatigue.

I had energy to spare when I finished my shopping. Then I found a checkout line with only two carts in it. The young woman at the register chirped a friendly "Hi!" to me and we chatted about the weather. As I picked up one bag of groceries, the handle broke. I about fell over when she stopped scanning, opened another bag, and helped me put the broken bag into it. I have never experienced something like that at Walmart before. And then I wheeled my goods to my car, loaded them in, and made the pleasant drive back home. I unloaded my groceries and put them away, and then did not need to sit on the couch for an hour to recover.

Last night, at the Brownsburg Walmart, I got a serious glimpse of why people move to the suburbs.

10 September 2007

A leader's character

A long time ago I had a creative job with an energetic entrepreneurial division of a large global firm. They made a killer product that had lots of buzz and made lots of money. When I interviewed for the job, my future bosses told me that their product's high quality is what made it sell, that my position would be key to delivering that quality, and that they would make sure I had the resources I needed for my work. They said I'd even have my own office, because they believed that in a quiet workspace I could really sweat the details and produce my best work.

I had spent my career doing more with less. Their promises charmed me so much that I was unfazed when they said, in the interest of full disclosure, that the CEO would soon defend himself against sexual harassment charges a former employee had leveled.

The suit settled as I joined the company, but if anybody said anything to me about the terms I didn't hear them. I was too busy happily immersing myself in my work. I had tremendous autonomy and was trusted to shape the company's products. The tight deadlines only made me sharper. I turned to my smart and focused colleagues for ideas, and those conversations always energized me. I also made connections with interesting people all over the country, some of whom rose to fame and fortune because of our wildly successful product.

The charismatic CEO frequently flew in from the home office in the San Francisco bay and always stopped by everybody's desk to say hello, calling us all by first name. He'd bring us all into the large conference room, bring in lots of food, and dazzle us with his big vision for the company's future and for the strong culture he was building to fuel it. The CEO usually brought his guru with him, a psychologist who specialized in coaching top corporate leaders.

The two had developed a list of ten core values around teamwork, quality, and work ethic that were supposed to be the platform for that culture. The CEO always asked us to quote from the values and gave prizes for getting them right.

The money kept pouring in. We tripled the number of employees in eighteen months. The CEO hand-delivered generous bonus checks to everyone that Christmas, and offered a few kind words about specific projects each of us had worked on.

The CEO visited one day to talk about extending the product line, and a huge number of projects it would bring. It seemed to me that this would dilute and devalue the brand, but he had always been right so far, so I went with it. My workload jumped; soon it was double, and then it was triple. I found myself routinely working 60-hour weeks and sometimes more, the quality and timeliness of my work suffering just so I could go home and have a couple hours with my family at night. Local management began watching us closely, calling us on the carpet for the smallest missteps. My autonomy eroded; soon I was only shepherding a rigid process. These things stood in contrast to the core values, which were still preached. People started to grumble; those who grumbled too loud were escorted to the door.

Material costs rose and the extended product line didn't sell as well as before. Stiff cost controls crept in. Christmas bonuses dwindled and raises became paltry. The CEO all but stopped visiting. He was said to be busy on endless sales calls – and I kept hearing troubling stories of extravagance, booze, and sex on these trips while the rest of us were left to do more with less. The CEO sent a series of lesser executives to keep tabs on us, creepy men who made the hair on my neck stand on end.

Then, the last Christmas I worked there, the CEO came to the office to hand out tiny bonus checks with the a look in his eye like my addicted uncle used to get when he'd been snorting God knows what. He couldn't remember my name and praised me for a project

I hadn't worked on.

What had been an energizing workplace had become a culture of fear and control. I denied it for months, but the intense pressure never let up. I reached my limit on one particularly ugly project. I worked late into the night for weeks trying to save it, but ended up delivering subpar work. I couldn't deny the changes any more, and I quit in exhaustion and defeat. I took a lesser job with a tiny division of another well-known global firm, relieved to retreat into obscurity and reduced responsibility. Most of my former colleagues, equally miserable, soon escaped as well; even the CEO's guru moved on.

A few years later, amid news stories of then-President Bill Clinton's challenges with the truth, the guru wrote an article for *Inc.* about the consequences when a leader lives a hypocrite's life. He named no names, but he clearly wrote about this CEO. In it, he wrote that the CEO had actually sexually harassed that subordinate and convinced his entire executive team to say in court that he had not. Reading it picked at my scabs. I had previously blamed all of management for how badly things turned out, but after reading this article I could see that the blame rested solely on the CEO's shoulders. Any man who would lie in court about his behavior, because only profits mattered, had to be the root of all that was wrong with that company.

The other day, looking at my LinkedIn network, I was surprised to see this CEO suggested as someone I might know. He now holds a high leadership position in another large, global company.

I Googled his name and that company's name and one of the first few results mentioned that he was named as a defendant in a lawsuit alleging sexual misconduct, harassment and intimidation, and internal office sabotage among his executives. The suit even mentioned a particular sex toy. I was not shocked to learn that there has been high turbulence and turnover in the business units he led there. I *was* shocked to learn that he was just promoted.

I'm left to conclude that this CEO was right. His character hasn't mattered, just his ability to bring profits. I feel sorry for the people who work under him.

15 October 2008

Checking my barometer

A large barometer used to hang on the wall in my grandparents' home. Grandpa tried to explain to me how it told him when storms were coming, which was important when you lived in the country and there were no 24-hour TV weather channels yet. It went over my head then. But after I grew up, my dog helped me understand.

About ten years ago, my wife brought home a dog she found shivering in some bushes behind the Shell station around the corner. We already had two dogs and three cats, but because her heart knows no bottom for an animal in need, Gracie joined the menagerie.

Gracie showed signs of having been abused. We figured her abuser had been a man because she warmed right up to my wife but cringed if I as much as shifted in my easy chair – and tucked her tail and ran when I stood up. As my wife and Sugar, our Rottweiler, helped her find her place in our home, her security increased, and she came to be less skittish around me.

I got our dogs after the divorce, and Gracie had trouble making the transition. I had to leave her home alone all day while I worked, and she took to destroying things in my house while I was gone. When I was at my wits' end, the vet said it was separation anxiety and prescribed Prozac, which helped. But I could see she needed a lot of structure so she could know all was well. I started taking the dogs on daily walks, made more time to play with them in the yard, and implemented solid and consistent discipline. It was, and remains, a lot of work, but Gracie responded well and became fully my dog in the process.

Gracie's security had just returned when Sugar died. I worried that Gracie would falter without her constant companion, but soon she stopped looking around the house for Sugar and instead just seemed thrilled to have me all to herself. But six weeks later Gracie just fell apart. She started destroying things in the house again when I was gone; when I was home, she followed me everywhere, whining and crying.

At first I thought that perhaps it sunk in that Sugar wasn't coming home, but then I connected some dots. I'm a busy dude, often busier than I like to be. Not only was I mourning Sugar after she died, but I was super busy for several weeks afterward. I had let up on Gracie's walks, stopped playing with her in the yard, and had relaxed the discipline. A couple weeks later, my own usual stress symptoms emerged: I was tired all the time, my shoulders and neck were stiff and sore, and I was irritable. I hadn't been getting to bed on time, I hadn't been eating well, and I hadn't been setting aside any quiet time.

I realized that I have a barometer, and her name is Gracie. She's a very sensitive instrument who knows that I'm off my game well before I do. If I'm taking good care of her, then I'm taking good care of me, and we're both happy. But every time she whines and cries when I come home and becomes jumpy, I always find that both of us need more attention. As soon as I give it to us, she rebounds, and I keep stress from piling up on me.

28 November 2008

Faith

When I became a Christian I was mistaken. I thought faith was a way to make my life more certain. Trust and obey, and all will be well.

It wasn't true. My wife and I were on shaky ground already when we both made the choice to follow Jesus, and our marriage only got worse from there. Toward the end, in my prayers I *begged* God to heal our marriage. He didn't.

When my wife filed for divorce, my pain turned to fury. I couldn't believe that God hadn't intervened to save us! I could have walked away from faith for it, but I'm a stubborn man. I was determined to hold God to what I believed were his promises to me. I went searching for them in the Bible, intending fully to hold God to them as I found them.

But through that study I came to see that God doesn't interfere with anyone's free will, even if what they're doing is hurting others or themselves. To do so would make their will not free. I also caught a glimpse of how much it tears God's heart in two when he watches us hurt others or ourselves. I slowly realized that God hurt for me, and wanted me to reach out to him so he could give me strength and comfort.

That's just what happened. I felt the ache, the rage slowly ebb.

My blog has always been about whatever I'm doing and am interested in. In my blog's early years I taught Sunday school at my church, and I adapted many of my lessons into blog posts. Trouble is, I wrote them for an audience of Christians. If you don't follow Jesus, they probably come across as preachy, as if I have all the answers. I regret that.

Today when I write about my faith, I try to show it as the imperfect work in progress it is. But this is where I was in my faith journey in my blog's first two years. Then as now, I was trying to find my way in my faith, and this is how I chose to do it.

Not-so-instant gratification

This was the first post on my blog.

Life deals serious difficulties to everyone. Losing a child, chronic illness or pain, injustice, infidelity, loneliness, addiction, and divorce – have any of these touched you? Do you have other equally difficult stories to tell? Expect slow and painful recovery from such things.

I've had plenty of serious difficulties in the past several years, including a brutal divorce that left me no longer living with my children every day. Things are getting better, but the path has been crooked. After a few good days, another wave of grief hits. I've learned that these waves are part of healing.

But I don't want to experience them! I find it helpful sometimes to distract myself for a short while so I can come back refreshed and better able to cope. Maybe I'll buy myself something small, or eat something I really enjoy, or rent a movie.

It's possible to turn such things into a crutch, using them impulsively and compulsively to avoid the pain. I've taken to eating entire large pizzas. Thank goodness for my blast-furnace metabolism, or I'd be a hefty man. A pizza soothes me for a while, but it's gluttony, and it leaves me bloated and uncomfortable.

This seeking easy, if temporary, relief is a form of instant gratification. But God asks me to wait for him to bring the strength I need to push through. Isaiah 40:28-31 puts it in a way that offers such hope:

> Do you not know? Have you not heard?
> The Lord is the everlasting God, the Creator of the ends

of the earth.
He will not grow tired or weary, and his understanding
no one can fathom.
He gives strength to the weary and increases the power
of the weak.
Even youths grow tired and weary, and young men
stumble and fall; but those who hope in the Lord will
renew their strength.
They will soar on wings like eagles; they will run and
not grow weary, they will walk and not be faint.

But that's so hard! How long do I have to wait? Days? Months? Years? Am I supposed to just lie around doing nothing while I wait for God to magically heal me?

I have figured out that we wait as long as it takes for God to use it to shape us for his service. The process of waiting, of enduring, strengthens us.

I have also learned is that God gave us our abilities for a reason, and he intends for us to use them to help ourselves. All of us can pay attention to the basics of caring for ourselves and build support networks of people we trust who care about us and will pray for us. If you're sick or in pain, you can go to the doctor. If you're lonely, you can get involved with something you enjoy – a church group or a hobby group – or volunteer for something you believe in. If you're grieving, you can read books about grief and join a loss support group. If you're addicted, you can start 12-step recovery. If you're any of these things, you can get a therapist.

Even when we are at the end of our rope, God is working in our lives to bring us greater peace, strength, and joy, if we'll just wait for it.

A woman I know went into the hospital for a hip replacement and contracted a terrible infection. She lay in the hospital, with no hip, for more than a year. It was brutally difficult for her most of the time, lying in bed day in and day out, tethered to a machine that dripped powerful medicine into her hip socket. She told me she felt like a prisoner. She couldn't do anything without help, and she fought daily to keep her low morale from collapsing entirely. That time finally ended, way past the point I thought a merciful God would allow. But everyone who knows her can see how she is remarkably more confident and poised. She resolved to wait. She had no choice, really. In my opinion it let God work in her to cause her to grow. As Paul wrote in Philippians 1:6, "[I am] confident of this, that he who began a good work in you will carry it on to completion until the day of Christ Jesus." And as James wrote in James 1:2-4, "Consider it pure joy, my brothers and sisters, whenever you face trials of many kinds, because you know that the testing of your faith produces perseverance. Let perseverance finish its work so that you may be mature and complete, not lacking anything."

When you look for the quick fix or the easy out, you could be robbing God of the opportunity to shape you to build your character to be more and more like Christ. Trust that at the worst times God is close to you, waiting for you to turn to him.

7 February 2007

Holding up my hand

The house I lived in when I was in Kindergarten

On my first day of Kindergarten, my mother walked with me the half mile to school so I'd know the way. I felt anxious about the long walk, but also reassured that Mom was taking me there. When the time came, I held my hand up for her to grasp and we left our house. In the warm September sun we walked uphill past the houses that curved along our narrow street. She led me along the Secret Sidewalk, a shortcut between some houses that emptied onto another street that led down the other side of the hill. As we passed the synagogue, Mom explained how Jews in our area walked to services there every Saturday. As we passed a patch of little sumac trees, Mom warned me not to touch them because they were poisonous. As we passed a wooded lot, Mom warned me to stay on the sidewalk because the hippies liked to hang out in there and she wasn't sure they were safe. As we rounded the corner and passed the Church of Christ, Mom said that I was not to join the other kids if they shortcut through their property. I took in everything Mom said, fascinated and excited by how much there was to know about this walk to school. When we reached the corner across from the school, Mom explained how to watch and listen for the crossing guard. The guard gave the okay, and we crossed and walked up to the school. Mom left me at the door with a kiss, a hug, and a promise that she'd be waiting at that door when school let out. I felt secure as I walked inside.

On my own twenty years later, I felt alone and lost. I wanted a path to follow that would work better than what I had come up with. I felt sure God would have that path, so I wound up in a Methodist church. The pastor sprinkled water on my head and I was in. I did things I thought I should do as a Christian: I attended Sunday school and services every week, I tried to quit swearing and always be honorable, and I helped with the youth group. I enjoyed the people and socialized heavily with my Sunday school class. But I struggled with God, whom I expected to judge me, eyebrow arched and lips pursed, each time I slipped up.

I also struggled to understand the church's rituals. For example, every couple months we took communion. We read puzzling texts from the hymnal and then lined up to eat a little wafer and drink a sip of grape juice. But I didn't know what it was for! I used to pray, "Lord, I don't know why I'm doing this, but I pray that you will bless it anyway." God and church weren't making sense. In time, I had some serious brushes with church politics. It turned me off and I fell away. I used to blame the Methodists, but something the pastor said to me many times comes back to me now: "Each man must find his own path to God." I sure wasn't searching so I might find; I guess I expected the church to show me.

One day, the Jehovah's Witnesses knocked on the door and promised that my Bible could be an open book to me, giving me accurate knowledge of God and His standards for me and for His people, the true Christians. I was nervous because of the Witnesses' notoriety, but the fun young couple who came to study with my wife and me soon melted those reservations. Steve, a slight man who bobbed and twitched with nervous energy, enthusiastically shared his knowledge. He flipped rapidly through his Bible looking for verses that answered our questions. In counterpoint, Jessica sat like a reference librarian, placid and poised with a heaping gob of thick blonde hair usually pulled up into a bun and glasses perched on the end of her nose. She could clarify in ten words anything Steve said in a hundred, but she always quietly let her husband speak. My wife and I enjoyed their company and our study. We became excited and encouraged to find that the Bible could be our sole guide to living a life worthy of the name Christian. At last, here's the path I didn't find in the Methodist church! It would be all spelled out for me! I could put on Christ like a new suit of clothes and leave my troubled life behind! But it troubled me that the Watchtower Society's theology and doctrine didn't always add up. Finally, Steve couldn't explain a particular doctrinal point to our satisfaction, and we began to lose our confidence. A succession of church elders came to try to explain. Finally one elder brought it all into focus for me when he said, "Look, just come to services for a few months, and then you'll understand and it will seem natural." In other words, he wanted us to become a part of their culture, and then we would naturally do whatever the Watchtower Society asked of us. That seemed flat wrong. We ended our studies with Steve and Jessica, and since we had turned away from their faith, they couldn't see us anymore. We missed them.

Not daunted in finding God's sure path for us, we found the Church of Christ. Dedicated to following the New Testament pattern for living a Christian life, they looked only to Scripture for their authority and not to any man-made organization. Since part of that pattern required baptism by immersion, my earlier baptism by sprinkling didn't count. The preacher dunked me, my sins were washed away, and I was in. We did things we thought Christians should do: my wife taught Bible class for children, I created a Web site for the church, and we faithfully attended twice on Sunday and every Wednesday evening.

On the one hand, I felt secure in the standards for Christians that the Bible seemed to spell out. Forgive. Love your wife as Christ loved the church; that is, sacrificially. Do not divorce, except for adultery. Give as you purpose in your heart, as you have prospered. Above all, do not forsake the assembly of Christians. I just had to do these things, and others the Bible specified, to be right with God. This was the way I was looking for.

On the other hand, I felt secret shame that I could meet few of these standards well and consistently. I didn't feel good enough. Truly, because of how much I missed the mark I often doubted my salvation. I compared myself to all the longtime members, most of whom grew up in that congregation, who seemed to be able to do all of these things. Seemed. Much later I saw how many of them had the same secret shame I did.

Shame's brother is fear, which led to members interpreting the Bible ultra-conservatively to be on the safe side. We practiced only what the New Testament specifically authorized. It led us to have some distinctive practices that included singing a cappella, and not celebrating Christmas. Hairsplitting doctrinal discussions were common. I remember a discussion with a fellow about church leadership. The Bible says that an elder should have children. (Look it up in 1 Timothy 3:4 and Titus 1:7.) My friend asserted that a man with only one child should not seek the eldership, just to be safe, because God might really have meant two or more children. "Oh, come now!" I said. "If you had one child and I asked how many children you had, would you say, 'I don't have children, but I have a child?' How absurd!" Yet he held fast to his fear-based conclusion lest he find himself hellbound.

But I loved those people. They showed my family love during a particularly painful and difficult period of my life. Several men stepped up to encourage me, pray with me, and study with me. Several women reached out to support my wife through the crisis. But a year or so later, fear seemed to seal shut the doors of that love when the elders learned that the end of my wife's previous marriage ran afoul of the church's teachings on marriage and divorce. The elders considered our story, reviewed Scripture, and then met with us to say that God didn't recognize our marriage and we had no right to each other. They were grave yet deflated as they delivered the message; one elder looked physically ill. I felt guilty that this had burdened them so. But our situation had become serious because the church's teachings spoke of separating and never remarrying. I was distraught. I had hoped for help keeping my family intact, but all these elders could do was tell me their interpretation of Scripture and withdraw awaiting my decision of what I was going to do. When you live by the law, you die by it too.

Through my own study I came to disagree with the elders' interpretation of the relevant scriptures. We couldn't come to a mutual understanding, and so we left the Church of Christ. We soon settled in a Christian Church down the road. Soon one of the elders from the Church of Christ called to ask where we were attending. When I told him, he gasped, said, "Oh! Jim, you were taught better than that!" and quickly hung up the phone. Soon we received a letter signed by the elders telling us that by joining a denominational church, "denominational" meaning "any church other than the Church of Christ," we had left the faith. Members there were not to associate with us except to help restore us to the faith. As far as they were concerned, we were no longer Christians.

God disagrees.

Shortly after we started attending that new church, I had this strong sense that my family belonged there. I heard a voice gently whispering, "Join here." Today, if I may be so bold as to say so, I recognize that as the Holy Spirit guiding me. I followed that guidance, but I didn't understand it. This church didn't fit the approved pattern I learned about in the Church of Christ. They took up special offerings. Women led singing and sometimes read Scripture to the congregation. A piano and a guitar accompanied the singing, and some members clapped and raised their hands with the music. They celebrated Christmas. These practices were forbidden in the Church of Christ and made me uncomfortable. But I was determined to stick with it because I felt God led my family there. Perhaps my service to him might not be about certain worship doctrines. Perhaps he will make good use of a church even if it uses musical instruments and celebrates Christmas. I took the uncomfortable step of letting him lead me without knowing the way first.

The elementary school I attended

My marriage didn't survive, and I was dragged through a brutal divorce. Not only were church members a great encouragement to me, but both pastors met with me regularly mostly to listen and empathize, but also sometimes to offer a good word of advice, and always to pray with me. The senior pastor, who grew up in an ultraconservative church similar to the Church of Christ, taught and modeled a great deal about moving away from doctrinal legalism to grace, love, and a personal relationship with God. They helped meet my physical needs by letting me move into the church's vacant parsonage rent free while I worked through the divorce. I have even been on three mission trips because of this group, which has taught me deep lessons in service and in being served. These Christians helped me stand firmly through everything that happened while also encouraging me to grow spiritually.

Trying to find and follow the ready guide, the list of things I must do to live successfully and in God's good graces, failed me. I tried my best, but I always fell short.

You see, I missed the lesson when Mom walked me to school on my first day. The lesson wasn't that I needed to strictly heed all of the things she told me about along the way. Knowing about the sumac and the woods and the crossing guard were useful and important. But the crucial lesson was in the simplest and most automatic thing I did on that walk: I held my hand up for Mom to take. I trusted Mom to guide me to school. I didn't know where it was, how to get there, or what dangers I might encounter on the way. I didn't have to worry about it because Mom knew the way and she led me there.

I trusted Mom because she had proved herself trustworthy in my early years. Babies naturally seek to trust, but grown men are wary. Grown men even forget that trust is an option. I sought rules and regulations because they seemed sure. It took crisis to reduce me to surrender where I could finally hear God's voice and take that first tenuous step toward trust. As my trust grows, I am learning that as long as I hold up my hand, God will take it. He will lead the way, and He will tell me useful and important things about living. I will find life fascinating and exciting, and I will reach my destination safely.

26 April 2007

God grenades

Last night I drove home after nine from a late dinner with some friends. These are the longest days of the year, and even though it was after nine o'clock the sun was still out, and it was warm. I rolled down my windows and cut through Broad Ripple, an old Indianapolis neighborhood known for its shops, restaurants, and nightclubs. I cruised down "the strip" past the nightclubs to soak in the atmosphere. Loads of twentysomethings were out clubbing, the women in dresses that portrayed their shape to best advantage, and the men in loose jeans and drapey, flowing dress shirts, untucked tails blowing in the breeze. There were smiles and laughter, shouts down the way and across the street to friends, and men picking up their pace to catch up to someone who caught their eye. I felt a little envious of their good time.

I'm sure that many of them were getting drunk and that some of them went to bed that night with somebody they picked up. I didn't see any of that as I cruised by. But even though I would have stepped out in fancier threads when I was twentysomething than the young dudes do today, some things certainly haven't changed since then.

On the opposite corner from the Starbucks was a young man with a loudspeaker and a microphone preaching the Gospel. As I drove through the intersection, I heard him say that God's was the highest name in Heaven. He was preaching in churchy, Bible-y language as the twentysomethings passed him by.

I wanted to stop my car, run over to him, and shout, "Stop it! Stop right now! Do you have any idea what you're doing? Don't you know you are pushing these people away and giving them something to laugh about? Did Jesus carry a speaker and a microphone and talk to the woman at the well from afar? Did Jesus talk in the language of the King James Version to the man who couldn't

158

walk? No! He went among the people and spoke to them in their common language, reaching them where they were physically and spiritually. He loved them in ways they could feel! How is it loving for you to lob these God grenades at these people? Go be among these people and let the light in your life shine through! That will bring souls to Christ; what you're doing won't, ever."

I was a mile down the road, about to turn and take the bridge over the canal, when I realized I'd been angrily saying this in my mind to that would-be preacher, and that I had missed out on peoplewatching the rest of the strip. I felt sad for the clubbers in Broad Ripple last night for having one more reason to think Christians and Christianity are rigid and unloving. I pray that God will soften their hearts — and the would-be preacher's.

9 June 2007

Find joy where life is

In the few months before I went on the mission trip to Mexico last fall I started a new job, my divorce became final, and I moved out of a one-room apartment for a five-bedroom house. I grieved my marriage, tried to be a good dad to my sons as they grieved the changes in their family, tried to work hard to make the right impression on the job, and had a whole lot more house and yard to care for than I had been used to. I was busy. I was *tired*. Downtime seldom seemed to come, but when it did, I couldn't just relax in it. I worried about how things would turn out or I ruminated about things that had happened. To run from those thoughts I'd just find something else that kept me busy.

This was my third annual trip to the Vida Nueva mission in Piedras Negras, a Mexican town on the US border. The day after I returned from the first trip, my wife and I separated. By the second trip she had petitioned for divorce. With all my troubles, it was a blessing to go away for a week each time. We usually do construction work on these trips; hot, hard labor. I worked hard for the Lord each day and lay down exhausted each night. I liked how the work distracted me from my problems for a while, and I liked how giving all this effort for God made me feel closer to him.

On the long bus trip to Piedras Negras our trip's leader found me and said, "I hear you know about computers. We brought 17 computers that have been donated to the mission. Do you think you can take a look at them, maybe get them set up? The mission wants some of them in the preschool, and a couple in the clinic." I lit up. "Sure!" Having worked with computers for more than 20 years, I was excited to contribute from my best skills.

I reported to the preschool on Monday morning and started work. As the week unfolded, I ran some basic tests to make sure the computers and monitors were usable. Then I defragmented the hard drives and installed needed software. Finally, I installed the computers where they needed to go.

Working on the computers

The problem with this plum assignment was that there wasn't very much to do. My tripmates worked hard in the hot sun making a new building's foundation, welding steel beams for a roof structure, and wiring a building for electricity. I sat in air conditioning waiting for disks to defragment and programs to install on these old, slow computers. I had lots of time on my hands.

In the mornings, I tried to sit quietly and listen to the preschool. The teachers talked very seriously in their daily meeting before school started. When the children arrived, they laughed and chattered as they passed and moved to their classrooms in the distant corners of the building. Happy singing seeped through the closed doors. When it was time to play outside, they filed out single file, the only sound being of their shuffling feet. There was also one poor accident-prone little boy who wailed in the distance every day as skinned his knee or hit his head. All of these sounds swelled my heart. Even a hurt child's crying is a joyful sound simply because there's life in it.

Happy young man on the playground

After the children went home at noon, I took breaks while I waited for tasks to finish on the computers. I walked to a large gazebo in the courtyard, sat at a picnic table, and tried to pray, even though my mind wanted to worry or ruminate. I could hear dogs barking in the distance, someone's radio playing, and the breeze rustling through the trees, all of which helped me stay in the moment. When I felt the breeze on my skin, it felt like an intimate friend's comforting and soothing touch. The intensity of it filled my mind and blocked other thought. Whenever my mind would wander to my worries, the breeze would touch me again.

Coyote, a filthy little dog, spends his days on the mission compound, shadowing the staff as they work. He sleeps in the shade until it's time to move to the next job. When someone leaves on an errand, he jumps into the truck bed to ride along. Nobody pays any attention to him.

One day at the gazebo, Coyote came up to me for the first time. I could tell he wanted attention, but I didn't really want to touch his filthy fur. But soon I couldn't resist him and I scratched and petted his head for quite some time. He leaned his head into my thigh, soaking it in. After a few minutes, a cat came and rubbed himself back and forth along my back. I turned to scratch the sides of his neck, which he ate up. Coyote scrambled to the top of a picnic table and lay down all comfortable and content. I felt the same.

I finished work very early the next afternoon. I felt drawn back to the gazebo. I felt no hurry, so I took an indirect route to see the others working. One small crew stood on a school bus installing overhead lights in a tall garage, and a fellow welded beams while standing high in the scoop of a big John Deere earth mover. How improbable both scenes were! I came upon a crew building a credenza for the preschool's computers. They asked me to help them move it into place, so I did. And then I went to the gazebo.

The credenza and computers in place

Coyote immediately joined me. He came up to me for a brief moment, seeming to greet me with a smile and bright eyes. I was startled by the feeling that a trusted old friend had looked me warmly in the eye and said, "Hello! I'm so glad to see you!" He immediately lay down on the gazebo floor, facing a small herd of goats beyond a fence a short distance away. On this side of the fence, two horses grazed on what little grass was available. I felt delighted as their muscles moved under their skin and they tossed their heads.

Then I settled in to pray and asked God to show me how to stay close to him. I lamented to him how my mind runs and how I press to stay busy and productive. As I finished praying, another worker on our trip tore around the gazebo in an old van. He had been repairing all of the broken-down vehicles on the compound, and he was probably testing a repair. He aggressively drove back and forth in an open spot next to the gazebo. Though the goats were in no danger, Coyote immediately jumped up and chased them away. I was excited to see that this filthy, neglected dog had a job and a part there. My heart leapt; his excellent dogness brought me joy. I could see that his life was in greater balance than mine. He hung out with people and rested much of the time, but when his job called him he immediately ran to do it.

Through this experience I heard God telling me, "I'm over here, Jim, over here, not so much in all that work you come here to do. Don't forget me, don't forget to come outside and sit alone with me, because I'm out here where life is."

Coyote ran off, someone put the horses away, and the breeze became still. I could see that this time of intense pleasure and joy was over. I asked God to help me find the joys as readily back at home, because I felt sure joys were there, too, and I was missing them.

Receiving this joy lightened my load. The next day, I was full of good-natured wisecracks, and I kept finding myself singing the song playing in my heart. But despite my good mood, I suspected that I had not yet learned this lesson. I felt sure that eventually the crush of life would consume me again.

I was right. Again I find it hard to suffer a quiet moment. Again

I ruminate about yesterday and worry about tomorrow. And so I return to this story, hoping to find a new insight. As I wrote this, I have been surprised by how all of these blessings came when I first stopped to seek God. And so that is where I will begin.

22 August 2007

A cappella

Ten years ago my wife and I visited a little Church of Christ in a plain building that stood on an empty highway in a rural corner of the city. The warm and friendly members eagerly accepted us as guests. The service began simply with a welcome and a prayer. Then a man walked to the lectern and asked us to open our hymnals. We saw no instruments; I wondered if music was played on tape. No. He raised a hand, swung it down – and then everyone exploded into song, belting out the anthemic hymn *Hallelujah, Praise Jehovah* without accompaniment, in four-part harmony, at the tops of their lungs.

Unprepared, I raised my hands as if to cover my ears. We stood there stunned, eyes wide, mouths open. We had been Methodists, timid singers the lot. In this building, even the tone deaf sang out, the strong, resonant voices around them carrying everyone's voices through the rafters and straight up to the Lord.

I loved singing, and had I missed singing in harmony after I quit the school choir when my voice changed. Elated to sing in harmony again, I turned to my hymnal and its shaped notes and tried to keep up with the congregation in this song I didn't know.

In time I learned it, and many others, in joy that came from feeling a special bond with God and connection with my fellow Christians. I offered the Lord my best voice, singing directly to Him. But the congregation's cooperative singing offered God something of much greater beauty than I could create alone. Our singing helped me not only acknowledge and praise God, but also transcend myself to remember everyone else in the room who also sought the Lord. I even considered Christians in other a cappella congregations singing unabashedly just like us. I felt in touch with the whole body of Christ.

I found comfort in my travels by identifying with Christians through a cappella singing. When away on business on a Sunday or a Wednesday evening, I usually found a congregation and went to worship with them. I noticed many times that singing the bass part of songs with them was how others recognized me as a member of the church.

A cappella singing was no less than a doctrine. The Church of Christ was born from the Restoration Movement in the 1800s, which sought to restore Christian practices to patterns found in the New Testament. The movement's churches sought Biblical authority for all of its practices. Because the Bible does not mention using instruments of music in worship, the logic goes, instruments are therefore not authorized. I've heard some preachers say that congregations that use instruments in worship are sinning and face hell unless they repent, and that a cappella Christians should not associate with instrumental Christians because to do so implies acceptance of their practices.

Sadly, arguments over instrumental music have caused churches to split for more than a hundred years. When I attended this little Church of Christ, a vast Christian Church sat about a mile down the road. The two churches were one until they split in 1894, and I'm told that instrumental music was one of the reasons. I know a former Church of Christ in my hometown that lost many members in the past decade as it underwent a spiritual transformation, a portion of which included adding instruments to worship.

Such legalism fragments the church, despite Jesus's calls for unity.

In time that congregation's legalistic interpretations of the Bible pushed us away. But we still believed many of the church's distinctive practices. We looked for a congregation in another branch of the Restoration Movement and found one in a particular Christian Church. Their beliefs and practices are largely familiar to us – yet they have a piano, a drum kit, and a guitar on the stage, and all of them get vigorous use during Sunday-morning worship.

It took me months to feel comfortable with the instruments. At first, I worried a lot about my participation in singing because of the instruments playing. I have since realized that because I am where God led me, that He knows what he has asked me to do, and that He is in control. So today, I sing there without worry. Unfortunately, the congregation sings like timid Methodists, and so I miss the powerful congregational singing that helped me feel so connected to God and His people. I hope that one day God's path for me leads back to a church that sings powerfully.

12 December 2007

Wrongly imprisoned

I've had some things happen to me that were neither right nor fair, and all I could do was suffer through it. Perhaps you've been there, too, and know the anger and grief injustice brings.

In Terre Haute yesterday, David Scott was freed after spending 23 years in prison for a murder he didn't commit. Somebody bludgeoned an 89-year-old woman to death and Scott was fingered. Actually, he fingered himself when he falsely confessed to the crime in a horribly misguided attempt to impress a woman. But when exonerating evidence was found a few months after the trial, both a county judge and the Indiana Supreme Court denied a new trial. New DNA evidence finally found the real killer late last year.

Scott, who is about my age, went to prison as I entered college. Since then, I got my degree, got jobs in my field and moved up the ladder, purchased homes, and married and had children. Meanwhile, Scott sat in a cell. What a loss he has suffered. Certainly, Scott's foolishness created his trouble, but the system's failsafes failed him for over two decades. His life languished while mine flourished.

One of the things I learned while studying the book of Ecclesiastes recently is that life often makes little sense and that justice doesn't always prevail. Those who don't know the Lord must bear the pain, while those who know Him can find not only comfort, but purpose in their circumstances. And those who know the Lord always have hope.

The apostle Paul spent time imprisoned. I have to believe that Paul experienced anger and grief over his imprisonment; he was human. But knowing that God was in control, he came to accept his circumstances and continued to serve, ministering to various churches by writing letters to them. Three of those letters became books in the New Testament.

I hope David Scott was able to find some purpose in his adversity.

29 January 2008

Love paves the way

I once heard a recovered alcoholic tell his story. He was living in a shed, drinking every dollar he scrounged, and life did not look to be getting any better. He showed up at an AA clubhouse one day. "I'm not an alcoholic," he told the man behind the counter. "I just want to sit and rest." The man said, "You are entirely welcome to do that, and stay as long as you want. Would you like some coffee?" The alcoholic returned for several days, each day denying his alcoholism to the counterman. "I do drink too much sometimes, and buying booze always leaves me broke, but I'm not an alcoholic." The man always smiled and said, "That's fine. You're welcome to sit here as long as you like." After many more days sitting there sipping coffee, he stepped into a meeting. He kept coming back, found his higher power, and got sober. He credits the simple acceptance of the man behind the counter, an act of love that paved his path to God, who freed him from his slavery.

Thirty years ago my brother used to get me to go with him to the elementary school's playground to play basketball with the gang. I was lousy at basketball and didn't much like everybody knowing it, but I was often bored enough to play anyway.

A group of slightly older kids, strangers to us, came to play one day. Their dark jeans, clean white sneakers, polo shirts, and neatly parted hair stood out sharply against our scruffy play clothes, dirty shoes, and messy hair. They were curiously overdressed for basketball, but they played well enough. When the game ended, stacks of religious tracts materialized in their hands. They said they were from the Community Baptist Church and they began to tell us about heaven and hell and how we had to accept Jesus Christ *today* or risk a tortured eternity.

I had never been evangelized before, and the pressure was high. "If you haven't accepted Jesus into your heart, if you died today you'd go to hell, which the Bible calls the lake of fire! You would be in the lake of fire for all eternity! Can you imagine what that would be like? Won't you pray with me right now to accept Jesus into your heart so you can be in heaven?" I was not going to be pressured and said no, I would not pray with him. He would not take no for an answer, and I eventually had to tell him to leave me alone. He wouldn't, so I ignored him when he talked to me.

I learned that Christians want to seem superior to you and use fear and pressure to get you to go to their church. I was now not favorably disposed toward Christians.

A few years later, a friend of mine asked me to visit her church with her. She said she'd arrange to have the church bus come pick me up on Sunday. I didn't know where she went to church, but I had not forgotten my past experience with Community Baptist Church when their bus pulled up. I felt on my guard, but everybody was friendly and the morning went fine.

Eight days later, however, three high-school boys rang our doorbell and asked for me. They wanted to know why I hadn't been to church the day before. I said that I just visited that one time with my friend. They said, "God wants us to worship him every Sunday. Don't you want to worship the Lord?" I didn't know what to say. I thought I had just gone to visit with my friend one time, but they expected me to come back every week.

I don't remember how I got them to go away. But they were back the next week, and I stammered through trying to tell them no. My dad came to the door and told them I didn't want to come back to their church and that they should take no for an answer. They came again the next week anyway, this time with an adult. Dad told them that if they ever returned, he'd get a lawyer and sue them for harassment. We didn't see them again.

When I went to college, I thought it was funny how you could always spot the Bible thumpers by their neatly parted hair, dark jeans, polo shirts, and clean sneakers. Did all Christians buy their uniforms from the same place? One of the so uniformed lived on my floor. I think his name was Mark. I steered clear as much as I could, but one day I couldn't avoid him and he struck up a conversation with me. Fearing high pressure, I stiffened and gave him one-syllable answers. But then I realized he wasn't talking about God or hell or church. He was just talking. After that I didn't work so hard to steer clear. He talked to me a few more times, and I began to respond in complete sentences. Just as I thought he might be all right, he said, "Hey, you know I'm a Christian. I like to talk about it with people. Would you be willing?"

Fear stabbed at me. "I don't know," I said. "I don't want to be pressured about God."

"Whoa, don't worry. I'm not going to try to push you into anything you don't want. It's just that I've found that following Jesus is pretty good. It's made a big difference in my life. I think it can make a big difference in everyone's lives."

We ended up meeting for an hour for each of the next several weeks. As I loosened up, I asked him questions about God and about his faith. He told me how it was for him to start on God's path, how he still messed it up a lot, but how God had been patient with him. He told me that God would be just as patient with me, and that he wanted me just as I was. He asked me about what fears I had about starting on that path. My fears were considerable, and I was not ready to give them up. And so our talks came to an end.

But as the counterman at the AA clubhouse did for the alcoholic, Mark made me feel welcome and accepted at the edge of surrender. When I was ready to take that step years later, Mark had given me a good idea of how to find the path God had prepared for me. Because of Mark, I knew that I should look for simple acceptance, because it was evidence that God's love was present.

Mark, thank you! I hope to live up to your example.

22 March 2008

The temple's grandeur

Thanks to Solomon's sins, Israel found itself exiled, scattered across Babylon. Jerusalem, and Solomon's glorious temple with it, was destroyed. But much later, as God said would happen, King Cyrus allowed interested Jews to return to Jerusalem and rebuild. 50,000 of them went back, and right away started work on an altar and the temple. The new temple couldn't be as grand as the old; resources were few. But soon the foundation was laid. Ezra 3:11-13 tells what happened next:

> And all the people shouted with a great shout when they praised the LORD because the foundation of the house of the LORD was laid. Yet many of the priests and Levites and heads of fathers' households, the old men who had seen the first temple, wept with a loud voice when the foundation of this house was laid before their eyes, while many shouted aloud for joy, so that the people could not distinguish the sound of the shout of joy from the sound of the weeping of the people, for the people shouted with a loud shout, and the sound was heard far away.

Many of these Jews were born and raised in exile and had never known the original temple. Perhaps their parents and grandparents had told them stories about the old days. It's probably safe to assume that they went to Jerusalem because they wanted to do God's work of rebuilding the temple and restoring worship. So finishing the temple's foundation brought them great joy.

But some old-timers had seen the original temple and knew its grandeur. It was clear by the new temple's foundation that the former grandeur would not be restored. They mourned what they had lost, and they cried bitterly.

I taught this in Sunday school a couple Sundays ago. A woman in her 80s said, "I know how the old-timers felt. I remember how worship used to be here. It was grand. I felt like we were really giving our best to God. But things have changed so much."

Everybody in the room understood. I wasn't there then, but I've been told: In days gone by, there was an organ and a choir and all the old songs. The order of worship was set, inviolable. Reverence and awe filled the room during that hour every Sunday morning. But things have changed. As older members passed on or moved on and their children moved away, membership dropped sharply. In response, a new preacher took the church in a different direction. Gone are the organ and choir and most of the old songs; in is a small rock band and several new contemporary songs. Gone is the sacrosanct worship order; now we mix things up to keep it fresh. Gone is the reverence and awe; now many of us raise our hands and dance and sway as we focus on the joy of experiencing God's presence.

Even though I was never part of the worship she remembers, I think I know where she's coming from, and I said so. I came from a non-instrumental Church of Christ, and that congregation could *sing*. When we lifted our voices as one, it was with such power I was sure we'd pop the roof right off. I felt that our singing really gave our best to the Lord. When I left there and came to this church, the singing seemed anemic to me. I still don't get into the hand-raising, dancing, and swaying that people do instead. I just keep singing out, and I'm probably the loudest person in the room. I badly miss the strong congregational singing we enjoyed in the Church of Christ.

But God made good use of the Jews' new temple despite its lack of grandeur. Not only was Jesus presented to the Lord in it (Luke 2:22-40), but when Jesus was 12 he sat among the teachers here, questioning them and hearing their answers (Luke 2:41-51). This plainer temple did not hinder Jesus' growth.

Then in John 2, Jesus gives us the proper perspective. Standing in the temple, having just run off the moneychangers, somebody asked him his authority for having done it. Jesus said in verse 19, "Destroy this temple, and in three days I will raise it up."

Jesus wasn't talking about the temple building. He was talking about himself. Jesus is the temple that matters. How we organize and execute the hour of worship every week is less important than how we carry out every hour the mission Jesus gave us. When we are in Jesus, we are in His temple, and we need to be doing His business under whatever circumstances He provides!

That doesn't mean it shouldn't hurt when changes come to things we held dear that we did for God. But we must stretch ourselves to trust Jesus as he sets the circumstances in which we work.

At my church, we appear to be growing again, and we're not robbing from other churches to do it. We've had several baptisms, all adults in young families, in recent months. Our hour of worship appears to connect with them. I'm not sure our old style of worship would have.

If these new Christians grow to maturity, they, too, will someday mourn practices they hold dear as Jesus makes changes that draw more souls to Him.

19 May 2008

Everything you need

Most of my life I thought I had to make myself right before I could approach God.

I had to stop swearing, stop having sex with my girlfriend, stop lying to cover up things I didn't want to admit, and stop eating entire large pizzas for comfort when I was feeling blue. I needed to meet my wife's needs better, pay more attention to my stepson, give my employer eight hours of solid work every day, and control my temper. I thought I had to change before God would accept me.

I had it backwards. What I didn't know was that I needed only come to God as I was. Then to the extent I kept trying to get closer to him, the more the things that needed to stop would go away, and the things I needed to do would happen. In other words, God took me as I was, but was not content to leave me that way.

I spent many years with my sins and shortcomings. Some of them I overcame by force of will, although I found that they tended to leak out under stress. Some of my sins I justified or minimized, telling myself they were no big deal. Some of my sins I could not stop no matter what I did. They were strongholds over me, keeping me in shame.

When those strongholds finally damaged my life enough that I had no recourse but turn to God for help, he took me in. In time, he cut those strongholds out as if they were a cancer in deep tissue. Although I can see he did it as gently as he could, it triggered consequences that hurt like hell. I don't know how it could have been otherwise; nor do I regret that suffering for the peace of mind it has brought. God has also used life challenges to bring certain changes in me. Finally, some changes just seemed to happen, and I didn't realize it until I looked back. I notice how calm I can be now.

I notice how much more easily I find happiness and joy. I notice how I increasingly can handle problems that used to baffle me.

You see, when you turn to God, he begins working to renew your mind, rework you in the image of Jesus Christ, and grow the fruits of the Holy Spirit in you. You actually start becoming the person God meant you to be! As I keep turning to God, he will keep working on me. I expect my serenity and joy to increase, even in the face of difficult times that surely will come. God will keep giving me everything I need to serve him and enjoy this life he has given me.

3 June 2008

Storm damage

I have been reading *God Calling,* a devotional written by two women (the Two Listeners) who believed Jesus was communicating with them. In one of the devotionals, they wrote:

> Turn out all thoughts of doubt and of trouble. Never tolerate them for one second. Bar the windows and doors of your souls against them as you would bar your home against a thief who would steal in to take your treasures.
>
> What greater treasures can you have than Peace and Rest and Joy? And these are all stolen from you by doubt and fear and despair.
>
> Face each day with Love and Laughter. Face the storm.
>
> Joy, Peace, Love, My great gifts. Follow Me to find all three. I want you to feel the thrill of protection and safety Now. Any soul can feel this in a harbor, but real joy and victory come to those alone who sense these when they ride a storm.
>
> Say, "all is well." Say it not as a vain repetition. Use it as you use a healing balm for cut or wound, until the poison is drawn out; then, until the sore is healed, then until the thrill of fresh life floods your being.
>
> All is well.

A thunderstorm rolled through last Friday night. I love thunderstorms and often find them calming. This one calmed me until about midnight when the lightning started to strike and the power started to flicker. Then, within a two minute span, the power went out for good, one lighting strike sounded awfully close – *pow!* – and then one second later, something hit the house – thud! It came from my youngest son's bedroom. He slept through it, so I went outside to see what happened. I found a large branch hanging off the roof over my son's room. Here's what it looked like in the morning light:

Not only did it twist the gutter, it punctured the roof in two places. I also found two other large limbs down in the yard, another hanging by a thread to its tree thirty feet up, and another lying across a downed section of the chain-link fence.

My sons and I got to spend our Saturday cleaning up the mess as much as we could. We filled four lawn bags with the small branches that littered the yard. Trying to remember what my insurance deductible is, I climbed up on the roof, pulled the limb off, and tacked a tarp over the holes. We also made a run to Kroger for supplies to get us through until power could be restored, which ended up being Sunday evening. Goodness, did we wish we could take showers, even cold ones, but the well pump doesn't work without electricity. But we made the best of it. I kept a decent attitude, and so my sons did, too.

I'm not dancing for joy over my punctured roof, mind you; this is going to cost me money and time away from work. But I'm surprised that I've taken this so much in stride. Where does it come from? I've done a lot of work on myself in the last five years, but this calm goes beyond that work. No, I have to credit God who reminds me that I've been in plenty of unwanted and difficult circumstances these past five years, and he's brought me through fine every time.

Another storm is rolling through as I write this. Let it rain. All is well.

6 June 2008

Purified

Finally, the wall in Jerusalem was rebuilt. It had been in ruins for many generations, but Nehemiah's tenacious leadership saw it rebuilt and thwarted many strong attempts to undermine the effort. Israel could not deny seeing God at work; after all, the wall had been rebuilt in an astounding 52 days. Jews everywhere responded by rededicating themselves to serving God. And on the day the rebuilt wall was dedicated, the priests purified themselves, purified the people, and then purified the gates and the walls. And then the singing and praising began!

We can't stand before God unless we're pure. The priests of Israel knew that; it was their job to purify the people of their nation. Jewish history to that time showed that the priests had their work cut out for them because the Jews just couldn't manage to stay pure. Nehemiah returned to Jerusalem several years later and found them having returned to all sorts of damaging practices that they had promised to stay away from. Boy, was Nehemiah ticked.

It's just as impossible for us to stay pure as it was for the Jews. This is why Jesus was needed, of course. The lamb of God kept the Law perfectly and bore the weight of all our sins on the cross, et cetera, you know the rest.

I once heard a preacher give a congregation a stern upbraiding about sin. He wrote this on a whiteboard:

S olution
T o
O ur
P roblems

and, with his eyebrows raised in that way eyebrows get when the person wearing them thinks they know better, said simply that the solution to sin was to stop doing it. Just stop! Stop! Yet I had sins I did not know how to stop, and they were crushing me. I wanted to stop them! But I kept returning to them and couldn't help it. I felt enough shame over it. The preacher's words only shamed me more.

What I – and, I wager, that preacher – didn't realize is that when Jesus cried "it is finished" from the cross, the whole mechanism of purity changed, and everybody benefits from it. Jesus has permanently purified us. If you've accepted Jesus as your Lord and savior and follow him, no matter what you do God sees you as squeaky clean.

Yet we still sin, and sin is what makes us impure in the first place. Romans chapter 6 makes plain that the purity Jesus gave us doesn't give us license to sin. We're to work at getting rid of the sin in our lives.

But what about that sin we can't get rid of no matter how hard we try?

One powerful way to look at sin is that it is the damaging behaviors, reactions, and attitudes that come from us trying to fill with things other than God our unmet need to have God near us. I wager that the sins we can't stop have, at their root, a core and maybe unconscious belief that our needs will not be met. So we keep trying to meet them ourselves. Usually, the ways we try to meet these needs aren't effective for long. Sometimes they end up hurting us.

The more we learn to depend on God, the more he will meet our needs. This is hard to accept if you believe deep down that nobody will meet your needs so you'd better do it. If you're like I was, you worry considerably about what you're doing and have tried hard, perhaps desperately, to stop. So I encourage you to do something that seems counterintuitive:

Take the energy you put into stopping your sin and, instead, put it into drawing near to God.

Yes, this means your sin will continue. That's okay for now. (Within reason. If your sin directly harms others, take immediate action to protect those you harm, up to and including removing yourself from the situation.) It's not that your actions are unimportant – it's that depending on God is so much more important.

This is a winding journey on a bumpy road, to be sure, and I can't draw you a map. But the farther you go on this journey, the more God will meet your needs. One day you will start feeling his presence and seeing him working in your life. You will begin to trust him. As your trust grows, your sin will diminish.

25 July 2008

Three good things

A couple years ago a friend sent me a link to an article (which I can't find now) about the virtues of thinking each day of three good things that had happened. We had both been recovering from divorce and joy was thin on the ground. She and I decided to try this exercise together, e-mailing each other our list of three every evening. I was surprised to find that on all but the most challenging days I could find at least three pleasures, even as small as "I enjoyed my cheeseburger at lunch," and recalling them actually relieved some of the day's pressures. But optimism never swelled in me, as the article promised, and I started to lose interest. I think my friend did, too, because our e-mails became intermittent and then stopped.

One of the themes of Ecclesiastes is, "Life is difficult, so enjoy the good things God gives you while you have them." The book calls out several good things – spouses, children, youth, food, drink. The more I encountered that theme as I studied Ecclesiastes late last year, the more I thought about the aborted three-good-things exercise. I decided to give it another try – but this time, I would tell my three daily things to God, since he gave them to me.

In these prayers I soon found myself grateful to God for each day's good things. Moreover, I started to see that God was there with gifts on every single day, and the more difficult the day, the more subtle – but sublime – the gifts. I started to feel like a child on Easter morning looking for hidden eggs.

Last Thursday I was driving home from a trip hiking through wooded and hilly Brown County with my sons when my car's transmission started to whine, pop, and grind. I wasn't sure the car would get us home, and we had 50 miles to go. I was worried about being stranded and about the repair bill.

But I also felt the breeze softly touching my skin through my open window and enjoyed the long shadows the trees and cornfields cast onto the highway in the afternoon sun. As the car rolled with the highway through the old farm towns, my sons and I sang along with the CD playing. I really enjoyed the drive even though the car occasionally popped out of gear.

Not long ago, I would have experienced and remembered only the worry. Looking for God's daily gifts has made me more receptive to them when they come. And knowing that there are daily gifts takes some sting out of the difficulties. My mechanic just called to say the transmission is fried, and that it will cost $3,000 to replace it. I'm sure God has hidden a gift even in this.

12 August 2008

Separated

Me and two other neighborhood kids walking up the hill, taken by the mother in this story from in front of her house. Judy Dieu photo, 1972.

When I was 5 or 6, I was at a neighbor's house a few doors down when a bad storm blew in. My friend's mother sent me right home. I made it down the path to the sidewalk when the wind came on strong. It blew me down the hill and away from my house as if a bully was pushing on me with all his might. My hair whipped around and stung my face. I called out, but I could barely hear my voice over the wind. I leaned in, pushed hard with my legs, and made slow progress.

Our house was maybe a hundred feet away and I could see light in the window. I imagined my mother inside ironing or vacuuming, unaware that her son was in trouble. I had never felt so frightened and alone, separated from everybody who loved me and could protect me. As I struggled against the storm wind, for the first time in my life I thought I might die.

The wind broke when I made it to our front path, and I ran all the way up it and through the door. When I came in, Mom was standing in the living room listening to a tornado warning bulletin on TV. She had heard the wind howling past the house and had just become concerned about me. I burst into tears and tried to explain what had happened as she collected me into her arms. We learned later that a tornado had briefly touched down nearby.

I can see now that I was not in mortal danger that day. The worst case was probably being knocked down and left to lie on the side-walk until the storm passed – frightening, but survivable. But as an adult I've been in much worse situations, some of which I've created and some of which were random chance. I've reaped serious earned and unearned consequences from them. Each of us goes through our own version of this. For some of us, those consequences do include mortal danger.

There are a couple ways to come away from the suffering these consequences bring. One is to conclude that if there's a God, he's not there for us. The other is to realize that life is often bigger than we can handle, and that we need a power greater than ourselves to help us through it.

God is always a hundred feet away, a light burning in his window, waiting for us to come home to him. Unlike my mother many years ago, he knows exactly what trouble we face. It's not God's way to ride in on his white horse or wave his magic wand to make our troubles disappear. He aches over our suffering, but allows it because he wants us to learn that life on Earth is not his primary purpose for us – life with him is. Through that suffering, if we choose to begin looking for God we will find him, and we will begin to experience his love, comfort, and even his rescue.

4 November 2008

The discipline of being real

I have had some serious stuff happen in my life. I have deliberately not detailed those things here because I decided early on that I wouldn't use my blog to air or work through my problems. I've written a bit about getting back on my feet after my divorce, about a bad storm that damaged my house, and about breathtakingly expensive car repairs. Beyond that I don't share here most of the difficulties I face, including times when my behavior falls very short of what God wants for me. Blabbing too much about my problems just doesn't seem wise. But on too many Sunday mornings I walk into church carrying the weight of these troubles and sins. I put on my smile, greet people, and say that all is well – and really, taking the long view of my life, all really *is* well and I hope not to forget that. But I still carry quite a weight into church some Sundays and pretend it's not there.

We fall into a trap where we think we have to put on our best face for church. We feel we have to pretend that we are more pure and upright than we really are, because that's what all of our apparently pure and upright brothers and sisters in Christ expect to see. And so we feel we have to deny our brokenness for at least these few hours.

> Let us hold fast the confession of our hope without wavering, for He who promised is faithful; and let us consider how to stimulate one another to love and good deeds, not forsaking our own assembling together, as is the habit of some, but encouraging one another; and all the more as you see the day drawing near. – Hebrews 10:23-25

Every time I've heard sermons preached from this passage, it's always been about why we shouldn't miss church on Sunday. I want to look at some other things this passage says to us instead. It tells us to think about how to spur each another to love and do good deeds and about how to encourage each other all in the same breath as saying that we should keep coming together as Christians. It does not specifically mention Sunday morning. We meet on Sunday perhaps because of tradition or because of Scripture or because the first-century church did. But that does not limit us to Sunday; we can come together at any other time. The point of this passage is that no matter when Christians come together, we should build each other up.

If you go to church hiding your troubles, shortcomings, and sins, how will anybody know how to build you up? If I don't know what you need today, I'm limited to offering general encouragement. Moreover, if you need to be built up because of the troubles and shortcomings you are carrying around, it will hinder your worship.

Let me say this in another way. It is important to learn to share our spiritual struggles with one another. This is being genuine among Christians. It is a useful and powerful part of accessing Jesus's forgiveness, which lets us worship in full joy.

Clearly, Jesus died on the cross to take away our sins. On that act our forgiveness and acceptance are predicated, and we receive that forgiveness and acceptance only through Jesus. 1 Timothy 2:5 says that there is one mediator between God and men, the man Christ Jesus. But he will use us in passing along his forgiveness if we let him.

> Is anyone among you sick? Then he must call for the elders of the church and they are to pray over him, anointing him with oil in the name of the Lord; and the prayer offered in faith will restore the one who is sick, and the Lord will raise him up, and if he has committed sins, they will be forgiven him. Therefore, confess your

sins to one another, and pray for one another so that you may be healed. The effective prayer of a righteous man can accomplish much. – James 5:14-16

I've heard "the effectual fervent prayer of a righteous man availeth much," quoted King James style, dozens of times; these are comforting and powerful words. But let's look at them in this wider context. These verses start by saying, "Is anyone among you sick?" The Greek word translated here as sick, *astheneo*, also means:

1. to be weak, feeble, to be without strength, powerless
2. to be weak in means, needy, poor
3. to be feeble, sick

Look at all the ways you can be sick – poor, weak, powerless, needy – and be included in this scripture! Many of our troubles, shortcomings, and sins are about being sick in just these ways. And then these verses say that one remedy for these kinds of sickness is to confess your sins to other Christians! But why is this remedy available?

So when it was evening on that day, the first day of the week, and when the doors were shut where the disciples were, for fear of the Jews, Jesus came and stood in their midst and said to them, "Peace be with you." And when He had said this, He showed them both His hands and His side. The disciples then rejoiced when they saw the Lord. So Jesus said to them again, "Peace be with you; as the Father has sent Me, I also send you." And when He had said this, He breathed on them and said to them, "Receive the Holy Spirit. If you forgive the sins of any, their sins have been forgiven them; if you retain the sins of any, they have been retained." John 20:19-23.

Here the resurrected Jesus appears to the disciples, gives them the gift of the Holy Spirit, and then tells them that he has given them the authority to forgive sins in his name. I believe that this authority is extended to us, as well. 1 Peter 2:9 calls us a chosen race and a royal priesthood; one of the functions of the Hebrew priest was to facilitate the forgiveness of sins by accepting sacrifices presented to God. He was just God's agent, and so can we be. This does not mean that we have the power to forgive sins, but that we can pass along Jesus's forgiveness.

17 November 2008

Your infinite worth

Mark 8:34 says, "If any man would come after me, let him deny himself and take up his cross and follow me." This verse used to really bother me. It sounded to me as though we were to meant to make ourselves nothing, as if we are all insignificant specks. I've never been able to swallow that.

Some Christians talk about this verse in just these terms. I've even heard Christians use this verse to justify letting people walk all over them or not following their dreams. "I'm nothing," they were essentially saying, "so I will suffer because it's what Jesus wants me to do."

I can't imagine that God made me with my abilities and interests only to say that I should not use what he gave me and be the man he made me to be. God didn't give birds wings and then tell them not to fly. But for years I thought that this is what it meant to be a Christian, and it kept me away.

I have since learned the great paradox of our lives: Each of us is of infinite worth, yet each of us is as common and ordinary as a grain of sand on the beach.

If you question your infinite worth, consider that God said that you are fearfully and wonderfully made (Psalm 139:14), sent Jesus to die so you could forever be close to God, and can and will have a deep and fulfilling relationship with you if you seek it.

But if we behave as though we have infinite worth, we come to think the world revolves around us, which naturally creates conflict. If we're together and I want lunch but you would rather sit on the couch and chat, we must choose. If the world revolves around me then we're off to a restaurant, but if the world revolves around you we stay home. Both can't happen at the same time. One of us has to submit to the other.

Mark 8:34 is really about realizing your infinite worth but not claiming the rights and privileges that go with it. That does not mean we turn down those rights and privileges when we do get them; we just count them as gifts. And it does not mean we deny our needs. If we're hungry, we do eventually need to go have lunch. If need be, we can delay it for a while, maybe a long while, for the sake of somebody else. Eventually we just have to eat! But meanwhile we can choose to submit to others for their sake.

Another way to look at this is that in submission, we let go of things having to be our way. We don't retaliate when we're wronged. However, we don't lie down like doormats or choose positions where we lose. We may even defend ourselves when necessary. But when things don't go as we'd like, when we're walked on or taken advantage of, when we're flat out wronged, we don't get even.

What this does for us is it frees us at last to value other people – to recognize each person's infinite worth. And that's the paradox. In order for us to recognize another's infinite worth, we must relinquish the rights and privileges of having infinite worth ourselves!

This is what Jesus did for us on the cross, by the way. As the son of God, he had every right and privilege. Yet he submitted, for your sake, because he recognized your infinite worth.

8 December 2008

Unrightable

A friend has wanted to talk lately about the hard work of forgiveness, so I've been thinking about what I've learned about it over the past few years.

My ex-wife and I behaved badly toward each other and caused a great deal of harm. We had cast down the china teacup of our relationship and it shattered. The best repair we could manage leaked through its glued seams. It wouldn't hold and we came apart for good.

That experience taught me a lesson that seemed paradoxical at the time but is now so obvious that it's elementary: Getting over being hurt means accepting the pain. It doesn't go away as long as you deny it. It doesn't go away as long as you ruminate on it, where it builds resentment. Acceptance is the only way through; acceptance accomplishes most of the healing. As I worked at simply letting myself hurt – and it hurt a lot – the pain diminished and disappeared, and I came to no longer hold anything against that person.

Because I'm given to foolish fantasies of a harmonious world, I also learned a second, more difficult lesson. I always thought that when I forgave, it was to be as though the wrong never happened and that I should be reconciled to the one who hurt me. God says that when he forgives, he remembers our sins no more. He gives second, fifth, ninety-fourth, and seventy-times-seventh chances. It was hard for me to see that while God loves reconciliation, he also does not want me to keep putting myself in harm's way. Two people can simply not be good for each other. Maybe one or both have a nature that's toxic to the other. Maybe the number or severity of past hurts make it too hard to rebuild trust. Maybe their needs conflict in too many ways. So sometimes the best way I can care for myself is to let the other person go. I'm sure that a few people are best off having let me go, too.

18 December 2008

About Jim Grey

Damion Grey photo, 2007

I keep going. I'm not sure what drives me, whether stubbornness or fear of death or an abiding faith that the future will be great. Some of all of these I suppose.

The worst thing that ever happened to me, the worst thing that ever could happen to me, was the end of my first marriage and the loss of living with my children. Home and family is all I ever wanted, and it torched me to the core to lose it.

I had to *make* myself keep going after that. To pull it off, I had to find meaning in all that had just happened – discover the lessons I needed to learn, and identify all of the positive things from past and present. I did that through writing these stories and essays.

Today I'm in my early 50s, live in Indiana as I have all of my life, make my living leading software developers, and have remarried. We have seven children between us. The empty nest is in sight!

Made in the USA
Middletown, DE
01 November 2022

13906153R00116